# HERSCHEL WALKER

## From the Georgia Backwoods
## and the Heisman Trophy
## to the Pros

# HERSCHEL WALKER

## From the Georgia Backwoods and the Heisman Trophy to the Pros

by Jeff Prugh
Illustrated with photographs

A Zander Hollander Sports Book

Random House ⌂ New York

*Library of Congress Cataloging in Publication Data:*
Prugh, Jeff. Herschel Walker: from the Georgia backwoods and the Heisman Trophy to
the pros. "A Zander Hollander sports book." SUMMARY: A biography of an outstanding
college running back who stirred up a national controversy in his junior year by quitting
school to "go pro." 1. Walker, Herschel—Juvenile literature.   2. Football players—United
States—Biography—Juvenile literature. [1. Walker, Herschel. 2. Football players.
3. Afro-Americans—Biography]  I. Title. GV939.W32P78  1983   796.332′092′4
[B]  [92]  83-4544  ISBN: 0-394-86163-9 (pbk.)

*Photograph credits:* Dublin *Courier-Herald*, pages 24, 107, 108; Gary Phillips Collection,
page 103; Michael Pugh, page x; Mitchell B. Reibel, page 119; Schuyler Reynolds, pages
41, 47; United Press International, pages 94, 109, 112; Perry McIntyre, Jr./University of
Georgia, page 79.

Manufactured in the United States of America   1   2   3   4   5   6   7   8   9   0

*For Terry,*
*my godson*

# **Acknowledgments**

The author expresses his appreciation to the following:

To Christine and Willis Walker and family, along with many other residents of Wrightsville, Georgia.

To coaches Gary Phillips and Tom Jordan, who helped mold a champion.

To Rex and Marguerite Jackson, Oscar Adams, Schuyler Reynolds, Kent Hannon, Joyce Leviton, Doug Hall, Gary Jones, Sam Skinner, Hank Leifermann, Lisa Rayner, Scottie Johnston, and Jackie Crosby, for sharing their observations.

To Sam Heys, David Davidson, Gary Smith, Loran Smith, Curry Kirkpatrick, Terry Todd, and Clyde Bolton, among others, who reported the story with special clarity.

To Richard Reuben, Elizabeth Siceloff, David Powell, staffers of the Atlanta *Journal-Constitution* reference room, and Claude Felton and Norm Reilly of the University of Georgia sports information office, for assisting with the research.

To Zander and Phyllis Hollander, who helped shape and assemble this book and offered generous quantities of advice and encouragement.

To friends, fans, players, coaches, educators, students, and everyone else who took time out to share their viewpoints and stories about Herschel Walker and the events that surrounded him.

# Contents

# Prologue

His name: Herschel Junior Walker.

He's a thunder-and-lightning runner with a musclebound 222-pound body that looks as if it were carved out of stone.

If Herschel Walker isn't football's finest runner ever, then he's right up there in pretty fast company. He doesn't carry the ball with the swervy, quicksilver moves of Gale Sayers. He's not a stylist in the mold of O.J. Simpson, or a scooter like Tony Dorsett, or a darter like Walter Payton. Rather, he more closely resembles Jim Brown and Earl Campbell—a total blend of power and speed.

"Tackling him is like stepping in front of a train," a University of Tennessee line coach once remarked. "It's like taking your life in your hands."

He's Superman in shoulder pads. He has a size 19 neck, has clocked 9.5 in the 100-yard dash, and has a manner that is refreshingly low-key.

He doesn't smoke or chew or spit. He drinks nothing stronger than orange juice or Gatorade. He stokes up on candy bars and hamburgers to go.

His strongest four-letter word is "team," and although he doesn't wear religion on his elbow pads, he credits God with throwing that crack-back block that springs him on third and 5.

He got six write-in votes for President of the United States when he was 18 years old. He once rescued an elderly woman from a smoking car wreck, and then quietly jogged away.

And in 1983 he made a decision that stunned the football world.

In a sense, it all began for Herschel in a moment of tragedy.

A small group of young men had gathered outside a tenant farmhouse as dusk fell in Georgia on New Year's Day, 1950.

They had been drinking and started to argue. Voices grew louder. Tempers got shorter. Angry words, like popping firecrackers, exploded into the quiet of a Deep South country night.

Suddenly one of the men raised a shotgun. He aimed and squeezed the trigger. The bullet tore through the chest of another man, about 30.

A few feet away a youngster named Willis Walker, then only 11, stood by, horrified. He watched his daddy fall helplessly backward, blood surging from the gunshot wound. Then his father gasped in desperation and tried mightily to stagger to his feet. But again he toppled over backward. Dead.

Soon Willis Walker, the only brother in a family of five sisters, would have to quit school to take care of his widowed mother. He would work for meager wages behind a mule plow, tilling 15 acres of cotton and corn—his anger and heartbreak bottled up inside him.

His mother, Nina Pearl Walker, would carry her sorrow through three decades—into the 1980s. "I'll never forgive that man for killin' my husband," she said. "He took somethin' he couldn't give back—my husband's life."

Willis Walker told each of his seven children about his daddy's death. He encouraged them to look forward to their tomorrows and forget about the yesterdays. Time, he would say, had healed the hurt he got when he witnessed the killing of the granddaddy his children never knew.

The fifth-born of those children had arrived one late-winter day in 1962—by coincidence, on Willis Walker's twenty-fourth birthday. Willis's wife, Christine, gave birth to a hefty son, who weighed 8 $\frac{1}{2}$ pounds.

Nina Pearl Walker, then widowed for 12 years, looked adoringly at her grandchild whose life had just begun. She asked Willis and Christine Walker, "Could I name that one?"

"Yes," they said.

"Could I name him after my husband?"

"That would be fine."

So the baby was named Herschel.

# HERSCHEL WALKER

From the Georgia Backwoods
and the Heisman Trophy
to the Pros

# 1

# "BO"

Willis Walker and Christine Taylor grew up born and bred Southerners, children of poor black Georgia tenant farmers who raised their families during the hardtime 1930s.

It was a time when much of the rural South was without electricity and indoor plumbing. It was also a time when blacks and whites were kept separate or segregated in public facilities. It would be more than a generation before the COLORED and WHITE signs would come down from the lunch counters, parks, drinking fountains, and rest rooms.

Racial segregation was also the law and custom in organized sports throughout the South. In 1940 (two years after Willis Walker and Christine Taylor were born) an Americus, Georgia, newspaper published an advance story about a football game between teams from two all-black high schools. As was then common, the article spelled out the seating arrangements: "A large crowd of white and colored fans are expected at this game. . . . A special section will be reserved for white fans."

Willis and Christine were born in Wrightsville, Georgia, and met as teenagers while picking cotton on Ralph Jackson's farm. They worked in Johnson County, in middle Georgia, where the Oconee River winds lazily through acres of cash crops, scruffy pines, and kudzu vines. The landscape is dotted by tumbledown shacks with tin roofs rusted by countless rainy days and nights.

The two youngsters fell in love at a time when significant social change was sweeping across America. In the spring of 1954 the United States Supreme Court, headed by Chief Justice Earl Warren, outlawed racially segregated "separate but equal" public schools. In late 1955 a black seamstress, Rosa Parks, refused to follow social habit and didn't give up her seat to a white man in a bus in Montgomery, Alabama.

"I'm tired," she said, refusing to move to the back of the bus (where blacks customarily sat in buses throughout the South). The incident helped set in motion the historic civil rights movement, which was aimed at obtaining for blacks the same rights and social courtesies that whites enjoyed.

At about this same time, Willis Walker and Christine Taylor were married at age 16. The wedding was held in a preacher's home on February 19, 1955, about two years after they met.

Willis continued working as a dirt-poor tenant farmer. Christine gave birth to two sons, Willis, Jr., and Renneth. Then Willis went to work for Rex L. Jackson (no relation to Ralph Jackson), who owned and operated a 750-acre farm that produced peanuts, soybeans, grain, corn, and cotton, about five miles outside of Wrightsville.

Willis made $25 a week. He also got a Christmas bonus of $100 from Rex Jackson, who gave the Walkers a corn-fed 200-pound hog to be roasted for their holiday meals. Willis drove tractors, combines, and other heavy equipment. He also performed a variety of other odd jobs with two other farmhands. Christine earned $10 a week as a housekeeper for Rex and Marguerite Jackson.

The Walkers and their two sons moved into a small tenant house with four rooms, a rickety porch, and a rusty tin roof. The house sat several hundred yards from the Jacksons' home, along a narrow two-lane road that stretches east from Wrightsville and through the Jacksons' sprawling farm.

Two more Walker children soon came along: Sharon and Veronica. By then, childbearing had become increasingly difficult for Christine Walker. Her third and fourth pregnancies had been complicated slightly by phlebitis, an inflammation of the veins. Phlebitis caused considerable pain and swelling in Christine's legs.

Meanwhile, as Willis and Christine Walker reared

5

their expanding family, they developed a special friendship with Rex and Marguerite Jackson. Theirs became a black-white bond that ran deep. "Willis worked hard and faithfully for me for sixteen years," Rex Jackson said. "The Walkers . . . well, they're just very special folks. . . ."

In the winter of 1962 Christine Walker expected her fifth child. Her doctor sent her to Augusta, Georgia, 60 miles away, for special treatment of phlebitis while she awaited the birth.

That year John F. Kennedy was President. He had championed racial equality and made it an important issue during his campaign. He declared: "The Negro baby born in America today, regardless of the section of the nation in which he is born, has about one-half as much chance of completing high school as a white baby born in the same place on the same day, one-third as much of completing college. . . ."

It was also in 1962 that John Glenn became the first American to orbit the earth. That same year Martin Luther King, Jr., and his followers met stubborn resistance by police and white counter-protesters during civil rights marches and sit-ins in Albany, Georgia.

March 3, 1962: In a hospital in Augusta, a town best known as the home of the Masters golf tournament, the newest-born child of Christine and Willis Walker drew his first breath. He was a healthy, husky addition to the Walkers of Wrightsville. His grand-mama, Nina Pearl Walker, called him a "God-sent child."

The baby was named Herschel, after his slain paternal granddaddy. Herschel was already a familiar name where the Walkers lived. Johnson County had been named for Herschel V. Johnson, governor of Georgia from 1853 to 1857. Johnson ran for Vice-President of the United States in 1860 with presidential candidate Stephen A. Douglas of Illinois. Douglas debated slavery with Abraham Lincoln, who, in turn, became President and freed the slaves.

In addition, the high school football stadium in Wrightsville was named after Herschel Lovett, a prominent local banker.

Young Herschel needed a middle name. His mother liked Cearneles. She changed her mind when a nurse walked into her hospital room holding the baby. The nurse suggested Junior, saying, "He just looks like a 'Junior.'"

Actually, the Walkers already had a Junior—Willis, Jr., their first-born son. What to do? Well, Christine Walker solved that problem. She made Junior Herschel's middle name.

At home, Herschel's brothers and sisters had nicknames—usually of one syllable so they'd be easy to pronounce (for example, Veronica was called "Nep"). Herschel was no exception. His mother dubbed him

"Bo." Was that Bo, as in Bo Diddley, the rhythm and blues star of the fifties? No, there wasn't any special meaning to the name Bo. "It was just a cute name to give him," Christine said. And Bo stuck—even to this day.

Maybe Bo was a lot simpler to pronounce than Herschel. Certainly it sounded less formal than Herschel, a name that apparently wasn't easy to spell correctly, either. At the hospital in Augusta, a typist misspelled Herschel's first name on his birth certificate.

The error apparently wasn't discovered, and straightened out, until Herschel reached his midteens and applied for a Social Security card. The official records listed Herschel Junior Walker's first name as "Hershey."

By her twenty-ninth birthday, Christine Walker had had two more children. Her sixth child was a boy named Lorenza; her seventh, a girl, Carol.

The small tenant house on Rex Jackson's farm became much too cramped for the Walkers' growing family. The Walkers moved down the road—a mile or so toward town, but still on Rex Jackson's property. Their new home was a slightly larger, much neater white clapboard cottage that sat on a gentle hill at the end of a red-clay driveway, which extended almost half a mile from the road.

Today, the shack they left behind sits forlorn and

deserted, half covered by brush and weeds, a reminder of poorer times. Rex Jackson now uses that house to store hay.

Once the Walkers had settled into their new house, Herschel Walker showed personal qualities that set him apart from his brothers and sisters. He was: A loner. A deep thinker. Creative. Obedient. Unselfish. Determined to be an achiever.

A light sleeper, he wrote poetry late at night, but he never wrote a list of Christmas gifts for himself. Mostly, he expected less from others than what he demanded of himself.

"The difference between Herschel and the others was that he stayed by himself a lot," Christine Walker said. "You know, most children always want something now, or they'll ask for something later. He never was that type of child. You'd have to drag things out of him. You'd say, 'What do you want?' He'd say, 'Whatever you give me.'

"In his own way, he felt he didn't want to be a burden to us. We always treated all our children equal. We tried to explain to him several times that he was one of the seven, and that he should be like the other children."

Actually, Herschel was unlike other children his age, as well as his brothers and sisters. "My other children would come in and say, 'Mama, I have a problem,' and then tell me different things," Christine went on. "But Herschel didn't. He'd come in and lie down. He wouldn't say anything. But I could tell, as his mother, that something was wrong. I would question him about it. And he'd say, 'Oh, nothin', Mama.'

"Most of the time, I'd have to hear it from somewhere else. Then I would tell him what I'd heard, and he would explain it to me then. He wouldn't come out and be open with Willis and me like the other children."

Herschel's mother is a pleasant, dignified woman who has battled pain and poverty for most of her 44 years. Her features are still smooth, and because of her youthful appearance, she is sometimes mistaken by strangers for Herschel's sister. Her eyes twinkle and betray none of the no-nonsense spirit that simmers underneath. What she lacks in a formal education she makes up with strong determination, an unshakable faith in God, and devotion to home and family.

Largely because of Christine Walker, life for the Walkers of Wrightsville was remarkably stable. Despite the years when they lived in poverty, she kept the Walkers a close-knit family.

She encouraged everyone else to push onward and upward, just as she rose from a $2-a-day housekeeper to a salaried supervisor of 38 workers at a local garment factory. In many ways, Christine Walker radiated much of what James Dickey, the noted poet and observer of Southern culture, said about the South. "Anybody who wants to learn about the South should get to know her women," he said. "They are tough, loving, frail and powerful. . . ."

Christine Walker was all those things—and more.

# 2

# OUT ON THE FARM

Wrightsville, Georgia, is one of those out-of-the-way places that looks like a scene from *Gone with the Wind*.

Most of the town's 2,500 residents go to work early on the farms or in the shops or small factories. They live in old frame houses built in the early 1900s or in drafty bungalows.

The city-limits signs now welcome you to THE FRIENDLIEST TOWN IN GEORGIA and the HOMETOWN OF HERSCHEL WALKER.

Life moves slowly in Wrightsville. There is time to stop and smell the honeysuckle. You can't go bowling or see first-run movies unless you drive to Swainsboro or Sandersville or Dublin, all about 20 miles away. Social life in Wrightsville revolves mainly around the churches, the electronic-game arcades on the square, the bus rides to and from school. As someone remarked, "The biggest thing to happen to Wrightsville was when they got the Dairy Queen and everybody would go there and sit on the hoods of their cars."

If you're young in Wrightsville, you achieve status among your friends by owning a car, being an athlete, or playing in the band at Johnson County High School. And then, you either choose to stay on the farm or to get away. Some youngsters go to college in Athens, some to work in Macon or Columbus or Atlanta.

It wasn't until the mid-1960s that the COLORED and WHITE signs came down in Wrightsville and in other Southern communities. Not until after President Kennedy was slain in Dallas. Not until after Martin Luther King, Jr., went to Washington and gave a speech heard around the world. "I have a dream," he said, "that my four little children will one day live in a nation where they will not be judged by the color of their skin but by the content of their character."

Today, although Wrightsville's schools are integrated, its churches and residential sections are not. Blacks (who make up 37 percent of Wrightsville's population, as well as about one-third of the 8,600 residents of Johnson County) live in scattered neighborhoods. One black neighborhood is called "The Quarter," a term that dates back to the days of slavery.

This is the setting where Herschel Walker grew up—close to God, family, and countryside, but far away from everywhere else.

13

When you're a child, five miles away can mean far away. Herschel spent most of his life out there in the wide-open spaces around home, five miles down the road from Wrightsville.

That means five miles from Outlaw's Grocery, Millers Restaurant, and the Dairy Queen. Five miles from Charlie Walker's Shell Station and from Paul's Bait and Tackle Shop. Five miles from everywhere.

"I love the country, where it's not crowded up," Herschel said. "You can get out and be free. That's where you get the opportunity to think a lot. Your mind doesn't wander off."

For Herschel, even a trip into Wrightsville was a rare experience. "Herschel never was one to come to town and hang around on Saturday afternoons," one Wrightsville resident remarked. "In fact, I've never seen him in town, except when he'd come in on the school bus. I've never seen him on the drugstore corner, or anywhere else, for that matter."

Growing up in a big family, Herschel learned to be patient and unselfish. Even the three-bedroom place where Christine and Willis Walker had moved with their children seemed to be filled with wall-to-wall people—two adults and seven children under one roof. In a sense, you had to take a number and wait your turn.

Like others in the rural South, many people in Johnson County work long, hard hours and want their children to as well. Which isn't easy now with so

14

many new distractions and conveniences like fast food, loud music, video games, and pushbutton gadgets.

Some families in Johnson County even look upon football as unnecessary. They want their children home after school—not kicking footballs, but plowing soybeans or picking cotton.

For their part, the Walkers always seemed to find room for *both* hard work and hard play. When Herschel and his brothers and sisters (and sometimes their parents) weren't running footraces up the long dirt road from the highway to the house, they worked on Rex Jackson's farm down the road. They did yard work, cleanup, odd jobs. "Herschel would work all day on this farm and never talk," Rex Jackson's wife, Marguerite, said.

In that part of rural Georgia many people say Herschel was "raised right." Christine and Willis Walker taught their children to worship God and always to do their best. Christine insisted that they exert "a hundred and ten percent" in everything they do, so that perhaps they might have opportunities that she and Willis never had.

Herschel sensed very early that his parents weren't as fortunate as others. So he tried not to add to their misery. "He wouldn't tell me if he was sick," Christine Walker said. "I'd have to take his temperature. I woke up one night and heard him groaning. I said, 'What's the matter?' He said, 'Nothing.' I looked at his arm and said, 'Good Lord, why didn't you tell us?' The thing was cut up so bad he had to go to the doctor. He never wanted to be a burden on anybody. . . ."

Herschel's strong sense of independence wasn't surprising to his father, who has worked long, hard hours most of his life. "I didn't worry about the boys," Willis Walker said. "I brought them up to work for what they got, not to depend on others."

On Sundays, Herschel would attend the Ranger's Grove Baptist Church and sing in the youth choir. "My family taught me right from wrong," he said, "and I stuck with that."

At school Herschel was part of a historic change in Johnson County tradition. Although the Supreme Court had outlawed segregation in the public schools in 1954, Wrightsville's schools were still segregated until the late sixties. If you were white, you went to Wrightsville Elementary and Wrightsville High. If you were black, you went to Doc Kemp Elementary and Doc Kemp High.

Desegregation was finally achieved throughout Georgia with relatively little turmoil. In Wrightsville, whites and blacks first went to Wrightsville Elementary together, then on to Johnson County High School (formerly Wrightsville High).

Herschel's sister Veronica was the first in the family to attend school from the start with white children. Herschel was the second. They and their classmates were called the Integration Babies.

16

Herschel began first grade in the fall of 1968, an ordinary year in Wrightsville, but a year of horror and change elsewhere. Robert Kennedy was shot in Los Angeles just two months after Martin Luther King, Jr., was killed by an assassin's bullet in Memphis. Thousands of young Americans were dying on the battlefields and in the rice paddies of Southeast Asia. Lyndon Johnson decided to leave politics, and the voters chose Richard Nixon for President.

Herschel's life at home was serene compared to his new world at Wrightsville Elementary. There, he'd never seen so many people in one place. No wonder he seemed bewildered at first.

While class was in session one day, the principal, Oscar Adams, was startled to find a first-grader wandering alone in the hallways. Herschel was lost. "The building had two wings," Adams recalled. "He'd been out playing during recess. He came in the wrong way. Couldn't find his teacher. I had to take him to his classroom."

For the most part, Herschel went through elementary school unnoticed. He was an enthusiastic student, but he struggled with reading. He took special counseling and, within one year, he raised his reading speed and comprehension to normal.

At home, the kid they called Bo often kept to himself. He played quietly in the room he shared with his younger brother, Lorenza. Sometimes, too, he sat alone on a hillside near the house, letting his

17

imagination wander. Out of such quiet times came a desire to write. Mostly, he wrote poetry.

Some friends attributed Herschel's quiet, private nature to his living out of town. "Maybe it comes from his family life," a friend said. "Maybe it comes from the feeling that what you do in your own family is your own family's business—and nobody else's."

Indeed, Herschel Walker and his family never once had to fuss with neighbors for elbow or breathing room. They've always lived out there, alone.

Even in poverty, they had one luxury—privacy. They savored their privacy as something special. Way out on Rex Jackson's farm. Way out there, south of town. Five miles from everywhere.

# 3

# VERONICA'S CHALLENGE

"Race ya to the house," Veronica Walker challenged Bo. "Betcha can't beat me."

Those were fighting words that even a chubby tyke like little Herschel couldn't resist.

Herschel huffed and puffed all the way up the hill. Veronica, a year and a half older, seemed to glide easily, like a speed skater. Again and again, she outran her slow, pudgy, and sometimes clumsy kid brother.

Sports were not something that consumed Herschel Walker during his early childhood. "I never liked sports when I was young," he said. "I never really liked to go out and play baseball or basketball or anything like that. I never watched it on television. . . ."

But if you grew up in the Walker family, it was impossible to ignore the spirit of competition. Herschel's first cousin, William Scott, was a superb running back and sprinter who would win a football scholarship to Clemson. Herschel's two older brothers would play football for the Johnson County High Trojans. Willis, Jr. ("Spunk" to his friends), would be a defensive end despite having lost one thumb in a gun accident. Renneth was on his way to becoming a fine running back. And Herschel's sister Veronica would win a track scholarship to Georgia.

The "Walker Yard Dash" along the long dirt driveway became a family ritual. Sometimes Christine and Willis entered the races and showed their children how it was done. "The only thing I didn't like about the racing," Christine Walker recalled, "was that we'd always walk down the hill and race *up* the hill." She laughed. "I felt *I* could do better running *down* the hill."

As Herschel himself would remember, "There was a lot of rivalry about who was the fastest in the family. It didn't really matter, because I don't think we really cared. We just wanted to have something to compete over."

Well, maybe it didn't matter then. Not at the start of sixth grade when, as one boyhood pal recalled, "Herschel was the slowest kid in our class."

But soon it did matter. Bo had had enough of finishing last in anything. His pride and self-esteem became important when Herschel turned 12. He was small and slender, about 5-foot-3, and only 100 pounds.

One day he approached Tom Jordan, a young man who coached the track and field team at Johnson

County High along with physical education classes at the grade school. In Herschel's opinion, Tom Jordan must have known what he was talking about. Jordan had coached Herschel's cousin, William Scott, and now he worked with older brother Renneth Walker. And both were excellent sprinters.

"Coach," Herschel asked, "how can I get big and strong?"

"Do pushups, situps, and run sprints," Jordan replied.

Herschel thanked him and walked away. Jordan had heard similar questions from other youngsters. The coach's answer obviously made an impression. When Herschel went home that day, he plunged into an exhaustive training program that he would follow faithfully for years. It would change his life forever.

While studying or watching TV—usually he did both at the same time—Herschel often performed 25 pushups and 25 situps, sometimes during the commercial breaks. He kept increasing the numbers until he could do 300 pushups and 300 situps. It was a routine he followed every day, along with a series of wind sprints—most of them 30 yards or less—along the sloping dirt driveway where he had yet to beat Veronica.

Tom Jordan didn't see Herschel very much during the summer. When Herschel entered the seventh grade, Jordan was "amazed at how he'd muscled up."

"How've you been doing?" Jordan asked Herschel.

Herschel smiled. "Just running, Coach," he said, "and doing my pushups." And getting faster and stronger. At 13 Herschel once playfully wrestled Jordan on a tumbling mat—and flipped him!

Soon Herschel's baby fat began to disappear. Thanks to all that exercising, he developed massive bulges on his arms and legs. His chest and shoulders filled out and he became unusually muscular for his age.

Still, Herschel couldn't beat Veronica in a sprint. But the gap closed a little each time he tried. His progress spurred him on. But losing every time to his sister frustrated him. Bennie Brantley, a schoolmate who would later play football with Herschel, remembered him vowing each day on the school bus that he'd defeat Veronica. "Tonight's gonna be the night," Herschel told Brantley. "This is the night I'm gonna beat her."

But then Veronica would win again . . . and again. And Herschel began to pray to God for a win over his sister. "I promised that I'd train hard and live a Christian life," Herschel recalled, "if only He'd let me get faster."

When Herschel's first full year of training ended, he might have felt like Sylvester Stallone in *Rocky* doing all that roadwork for the big fight.

Herschel had done more than 100,000 pushups—some from handstands, others on one arm, to relieve the monotony. He had done more than 100,000 sit-ups. He had run almost 500,000 yards, if you added up all those wind sprints—and subtracted the days when it rained and Herschel didn't run.

Tom Jordan, who now coaches track and field at the West Oak High School in Westminster, South Carolina, remembers Herschel as having been cut from a different mold than that of his peers. "The biggest thing I saw at that time was a hunger," Jordan said. "Now Herschel would do whatever was needed to accomplish the task that he wanted to accomplish. He just didn't let anything get in the way."

Herschel now had a rock-solid physique, developed partly by his strong determination and self-discipline. "My mind's like a general and my body's like an army," he would say years later. "I keep the body in shape and it does what I tell it to do. I sometimes even feel myself almost lifting up out of my body and looking down on myself while I run sprints. I'll be coaching myself from up above. 'Come on, Herschel,' I'll say to myself out loud, 'pick up those knees. Pump your arms.' If an army stopped training, it wouldn't take long for it to fall apart. An army needs discipline, just like a man does."

Just as Herschel grew taller and stronger, he also ran faster than ever. He was still a step or two behind a couple of his peers—and he had yet to outrun Veronica on the fast track at home. But now you could see the progress, and you could almost count the days until he would succeed as a sprinter in his school *and* in his family.

"By seventh grade, he was even with us," his pal, Milt Moorman, remembered. "By eighth, he was pulling away. By ninth, there was no hope for us. He was running 9.9 in the 100."

When Herschel entered high school, he played football on the B team. He wasn't old enough to play on the varsity with his brother Renneth, but he desperately wanted to play. "Mama," he said, "I'm gonna be on the same team with Renneth next year."

"Oh no," Christine Walker said. "Those boys are too big and too tough. . . ."

One of Herschel's coaches told her it was foolish to hold him back. "He's better than the team he's on," the coach said. "I think we oughta give him a chance."

By tenth grade, Herschel had moved into the starting lineup of the Johnson County Trojans as the fullback. Mostly, he blocked for tailback Wannie Cason,

**It didn't take long for Herschel to become a starter for the Johnson County Trojans.**

who gained more than 1,300 yards. But Herschel didn't do badly himself. He rushed for 987 yards, even though he carried the ball far less than the tailback did.

Some people thought Herschel—then about 6 feet tall and approaching 200 pounds—should have run from tailback and carried the ball more often. But it was traditional that starting tailbacks at Johnson County worked their way up. Wannie Cason, a senior, had a two-year head start on Herschel, a sophomore. The Trojans won 6 games and lost 4 during that autumn of 1977. The head coach resigned and a new coach, Gary Phillips, came over from Macon.

By the summer of 1978 Herschel had played varsity for a full season but he still had to beat his sister. Veronica now lined up against a muscular sprinter who had broken 10 seconds flat for the 100 and who would soon be the starting tailback for the Johnson County High Trojans.

And this time Bo won. He did it again . . . and again . . . just as he would soon outrun seemingly everybody in Georgia.

Veronica cried all night. She said she would quit track. But her mother said no, in her customarily soothing, but pointed, sort of way. She reminded Veronica about giving "a hundred and ten percent" effort. She convinced Veronica to keep on running and she assured her that losing to Herschel didn't mean the end of the world.

# 4

# "THE BIGGEST ARMS IN GEORGIA"

It was late summer of 1978. In the Wrightsville *Headlight* a fellow named Herschell Hall advertised worms for sale. Somebody put 1,025 hogs on the auction block. But there were some changes.

Christine and Willis Walker had left the green pastures of Rex Jackson's farm for jobs that paid better—she at a trousers factory, he at a mill that converted kaolin, a fine white clay, into chalk.

Now that he'd defeated Veronica, Herschel ran out of opponents in the family sprints. So he tried to outrun Smoky, a pet horse, all over the farm. Smoky was too fast.

Whenever Herschel and his brothers needed a change from racing the horse and each other, they turned to wrestling. The matchups: Herschel and Lorenza vs. Willis, Jr., and Renneth. Kid brothers vs. big brothers.

If tempers heated up, Christine Walker put her foot down. On one occasion she ordered a ceasefire.

She may have prevented a friendly skirmish of hammerlocks and toeholds from turning into assault and battery. "I think they were gonna get pretty angry one Sunday," she recalled, "and I stopped that, right off the bat—before it got too far. I told them to do something else."

They went outside and made up a high-jump event. The object: to see who could jump over a hedge—from a flatfooted takeoff. Next, they prepared a contest more suited for daredevils: a running leap over their daddy's late-model Ford sedan.

But their daddy wasn't amused.

"Hey!" Willis screamed at his sons. "I ain't got no money to put anybody in the hospital!"

Herschel very nearly *did* have to go to the hospital. He loved motorcycles. You could hear him from miles away, whenever he rode to and from football practice.

One day in 1978 Herschel sped along a dirt path on a 100cc Honda that Willis had bought for his four sons. Suddenly the bike hit a rock and skidded wildly out of control. The impact flipped Herschel helplessly over the handlebars. He crash-landed so hard that he all but gouged out a crater in the path.

When the dust cleared, someone found Herschel sprawled in the dirt and the bike tipped over, its engine still whirring. Herschel was bleeding from his head and ended up with a scar. He also got an order from his mother: "No more motorcycles."

But Herschel simply said, "If you don't take any

chances, you don't experience any thrills." He didn't give up his motorcycle.

There were changes at school when the Johnson County Trojans opened practice for the 1978 football season. They had a new head coach, Gary Phillips, and a new tailback, Herschel Walker. Herschel was a converted fullback who, at 6-foot-1 and 205 pounds, was bigger than most linemen he would face. And faster too.

Gary Phillips had arrived in Wrightsville with lots of enthusiasm and fresh ideas. One day in late August the telephone rang in coach Phillips' office. A sportswriter was on the line. "How is it, Coach," he asked, "over there in the sticks—in Johnson County?"

"Well, I think I've got a good football player," Phillips replied. "A kid named Herschel Walker. A junior who weighs 205! He's already run 9.8, as a *sophomore!*"

The nation had not yet heard of 16-year-old Herschel Walker. Nor had most of the state of Georgia. His name, for now, was pretty much confined to the conversations of folks who talked football at Bobby Newsome's Ford, or Millers Restaurant.

It wasn't until Herschel's junior year that his high school guidance counselor, Schuyler Reynolds, felt he knew him well enough to make an informed evaluation of him. As a student, Herschel was "probably an overachiever," Reynolds said, referring to his "good mind."

Herschel particularly liked courses that taxed his reasoning powers. "I remember his geometry teacher saying how much he enjoyed geometry," Reynolds said. "He seemed to like everything. He was an avid student. He tried to do well at everything he did. He was extremely self-disciplined. Not in all areas. I mean, everybody's got *some* weaknesses. . . . [But] I don't think his teachers gave him anything because of who he was."

Early on, Herschel began to realize the differences between growing up black and growing up white.

"I think Herschel was taught very, very early," Gary Phillips said, "the way many black kids are taught. They're told, 'You're in a minority group. Things aren't going to be exactly like they are in the storybooks.' They're also taught to ask, 'Who am I?' and 'Where did I come from?' Like it or not, our whole society is into that. We all look for some kind of identity. We can't be just a face in the crowd. We've got to have some type of status."

Herschel Walker would reach for status on the playing fields and the running tracks. However, when he played for the Johnson County High Trojans in 1978, he didn't wear a fancy uniform. Instead of regulation jerseys, the team wore oversized T-shirts that were slashed up the sleeves and cut up with holes.

If anybody tried to tackle Herschel or the other Johnson County backs by merely grabbing fistfuls of fabric, it was hopeless. The shirts ripped apart almost as easily as bathroom tissue. A Wrightsville factory had donated stacks of T-shirts to be scissored into makeshift tear-away jerseys. Stacks of them were kept in readiness on the sidelines, to replace those that became too shredded to be worn. "We really didn't have the money," Phillips said. "We just couldn't afford the more expensive tear-away jerseys."

For the season-opening game against the West Laurens County Raiders from Dublin, Herschel and the other ball carriers wore blue tear-away T-shirts. Each bore large numerals scrawled in white liquid shoe polish with a spongelike applicator. For games in which the Johnson County players suited up in white jerseys, the backs wore white tear-away shirts, their numbers hand-painted in black shoe polish.

So tattered were Johnson County's homemade jerseys that they sometimes appeared more off the players than on. "If one of these clowns touches you," Phillips told Herschel and the other backs before the game, "your jersey's gonna tear right off."

Herschel and his teammates were fired up. So was Phillips. He was, in his debut as head coach, matched against his old mentor, West Laurens coach Tom Wilson, who had hired Phillips fresh out of college. Wilson's team was young and inexperienced—and seemed to spend most of the game turning over the ball to Johnson County.

Moments after one of those turnovers, Herschel scored from three yards out—his only touchdown of the game. He also scampered 24 yards to set up another touchdown and finished with 11 carries for 68 yards. Johnson County won in a breeze, 26–0.

About the only question unresolved that night was how much longer Herschel and his backfield teammates could get away with wearing those ragtag T-shirts. As the season wore on, rival teams and officials complained to the Georgia High School Athletic Association.

But almost nobody noticed that Herschel also played well on defense—when tear-away jerseys didn't matter. As a 205-pound linebacker, Herschel was positioned against the opposing team's strong side, against the flow of its best plays and toughest blockers. Just as nobody dragged him down from behind when he carried the ball into the open field, nobody seemed to be able to outrun Herschel, the defender, either.

All told, Herschel made 11 individual tackles in Johnson County's second game of the 1978 season—against Wilkinson County, the defending subregional champion. Wilkinson grabbed a 7–0 lead on only its second possession, but after that fumbled and bumbled when Herschel and his fellow defenders began to make life miserable for the Warriors. They never drove into Johnson County territory again until the final moments, long after the game was decided.

The hometown crowd in Wrightsville also had plenty to cheer about whenever Herschel carried the ball. He hammered out 113 yards on 17 carries, mostly on quick pitches from the quarterback. A thundering roar went up during the second quarter, when Herschel dashed 27 yards on a sweep for the Trojans' go-ahead touchdown. Final score: Johnson County 21, Wilkinson County 7.

Actually, it could have been worse for Wilkinson County. Herschel had a 64-yard touchdown run nullified by a clipping penalty, and two other Johnson County touchdowns were called back. Before the season ended, Herschel would pile up a Johnson County High record 1,983 yards and 22 touchdowns—but he would be stripped of nine more touchdowns because of penalties.

The team's penalties and sloppy play, in fact, cramped Herschel's style the following week in Johnson County's first road game of the season—against East Laurens County, in Dublin. With the score 0–0 at halftime, Gary Phillips was furious. He chewed out his players in the locker room. When play resumed, Herschel carried the Trojans—and for that matter, a lot of East Laurens tacklers—on his muscular back. He ran 26 times for a whopping 207 yards and the game's only two touchdowns. The first was a 49-yard breakaway, the second a 3-yard plunge. Johnson County escaped with a 12–0 win and stayed unbeaten after three games.

Like his teammates, Herschel wasn't free of mistakes, either. Nor was he spared the coaches' criticism, although Phillips says their words were softened in Herschel's case. "Tom Jordan [the defensive coach] helped me a lot with Herschel," Phillips said. "He told me Herschel is one of these guys you really can't yell at very much. So what I tried to do was just talk to him. A lot of times, when he made mistakes, he knew he made them as quickly as you said, 'Herschel!' He'd say, 'Yes, sir! I know! I didn't do this, or do that.' And I'd say to him, 'That's right.' . . . Some kids, you just have to jack 'em up. Other guys, all you've got to do is just talk to them. . . ."

At practice Phillips often told his players, "We're gonna have the biggest arms in Georgia!" If a player jumped a snap count, or leaned offside, or telegraphed a play, or missed an assignment, the Johnson County coaches carried out an exercise that smacked of an army training camp. A coach would scream, "Jump down and give me 20 pushups!"

With Herschel it was different. Often, if he blew an assignment, he'd beat the command and say, "How many pushups, Coach?"

"Twenty-five!" Phillips would reply.

Herschel would promptly do 25 pushups—often on one arm. Then he'd spring to his feet and say, "Is that enough?"

"Do you know what you did wrong?" Phillips would ask.

"Yes, sir!"

Herschel did more things right than wrong against Metter High. One of Wrightsville's biggest crowds in years packed Herschel Lovett Stadium early in 1978 and watched Herschel almost singlehandedly rescue the Johnson County Trojans from the clutches of defeat.

Metter had stifled the Trojans for the better part of three quarters and led, 13–0. But then Metter discovered that even if you can stop some of the Trojans some of the time, you can't stop all of the Trojans all of the time.

First, Herschel broke loose like a runaway bull, slipping tackles along the way, to a 33-yard touchdown run. Now Johnson County trailed, 13–7.

Then, with Metter controlling the ball in Johnson County territory in the final $4\frac{1}{2}$ minutes of the game, a Johnson County defender smacked hard into the Metter quarterback. The football popped into the air.

Right there to grab it was Herschel, the strong linebacker. And away he went. The goal line was 60 yards away. There was no catching Herschel. He scored easily. Milt Moorman's second extra point of the night made it 14–13, and the Trojans went on to win, 21–13, and stay unbeaten.

Johnson County's football fans sensed that they had watched the start of something very big.

Herschel's running style prompted Gary Phillips to call him a "floater." "He floats and glides," Phillips said. "He floats, floats, and reads the blocks. Then he finds the alley, and then—boom!—he's gone."

Johnson County's strategy was clear: give the ball

to Herschel again and again. Wear down the defenders. And he would spring loose sooner or later. Even if he didn't break away, it would take several defenders to topple him.

Phillips says he believed Herschel could run even better, if only his knees didn't stay so low. "I always tried to get him to pick his legs up," he says. "I told him if he ever hit anybody with one of those thighs he'd kill him."

But neither Herschel nor his teammates were perfect . . . yet.

They went on to lose three games in succession. First, they got 113 yards and two touchdowns from Herschel, but they blew a 20–7 lead, lost the ball four times in the second half, and lost the game to archrival Bleckley County, 27–20.

Next, the Trojans traveled to play Savannah Country Day, an all-white private school, and lost again, 14–13. Herschel rushed for 112 yards, but fumbled to kill a scoring drive. He also intercepted a Savannah pass and ran it back 45 yards to a touchdown, only for the play to be wiped out by a clipping penalty.

One week later the Trojans returned home, and their record shrank to 4-3. This time they lost to Emanuel County Institute, 14–10. Herschel carried 19 times for 100 yards, including a 20-yard touchdown sweep for Johnson County's only touchdown. But E.C.I made him struggle for most of those yards, by putting up eight- and nine-man fronts against him.

The playing conditions didn't help, either. It had been a rainy, muddy night in Wrightsville.

EVERYTHING IS BETTER IN METTER. The Johnson County Trojans saw the road sign on their bus ride into Metter for their next game.

On this night things did get better for the Trojans and carloads of their fans who made the trip from Wrightsville.

Herschel and his teammates won, 13–7, but they had to pull the game out in the second half. For Herschel it was another blockbuster game: 164 yards on 28 carries and a 23-yard touchdown run for Johnson County's first score. At the same time Herschel ran his season total past 1,000 yards.

Now came a grudge rematch with Savannah Country Day back home in Wrightsville. This time Herschel & Company built a 13–7 lead by halftime and made it stand up for a revenge win. Along the way Herschel got 206 yards and scored two touchdowns. On one of those scoring runs, he smashed through the middle, broke one tackle, careened off six other defenders, and raced 73 yards down the sideline, in front of Johnson County's screaming rooters.

The Trojans also lost their tear-away shirts again—this time forever. Officials said the shirts had to go. "They told us we had to wear jerseys with some kind of iron-on Gothic numerals," Gary Phillips recalled. "Hand-painted numerals were outlawed."

In a rematch against Emanuel County Institute, Johnson County sprang an unusual formation that Phillips called "Super Splits." Trailing 17–14 late in the game, the Trojans lined up their guards two feet from the center, and their tackles 12 feet from the guards, which left monstrous holes at the line of scrimmage.

E.C.I., which had been keying on Herschel all night, was apparently caught by surprise. Fullback Jerome Taylor, one of Herschel's blockers, took a handoff from quarterback Edd Price. He romped right up the middle, untouched, for a 28-yard touchdown that gave Johnson County the Sub-Regional championship, 20–17.

It was a night to remember for Herschel. Not only did he score twice (on runs of 31 and 46 yards, the latter after scooping up a fumble), but he gained 182 yards to break Johnson County High's single-season rushing record. Herschel now had 1,424 yards through ten games, to say nothing of 15 touchdowns.

The next stop: the Region 3-A playoffs. No team representing Johnson County had advanced this far in 20 years—not since the days when all-white Wrightsville High played the only football in town and all-black Doc Kemp High fielded no football team.

With Herschel smashing for 169 yards, scoring two touchdowns from 21 and 66 yards out, catching two passes, and even throwing a 40-yarder, Johnson County trampled visiting Toombs County Central, 47–12.

Even Herschel's freshman brother, Lorenza, got into the act. He came off the bench and caught a fourth-quarter touchdown pass.

Now Wrightsville had caught something else—a severe epidemic of playoff fever. Johnson County had earned the right to host the Region 3-A title game— a third meeting with Savannah Country Day.

Johnson County High, an ancient building constructed of concrete blocks, was festooned with banners and crepe paper. The school had to lease 1,000 bleacher-type seats to accommodate the overflow at Herschel Lovett Stadium (normal capacity: 2,000) and satisfy playoff requirements of a 3,000-seat arena.

A deputy sheriff approached Phillips on the field, during the pregame frenzy, and handed him a paper napkin drawn with X's and O's and squiggly lines. "Here," the deputy whispered to Phillips. "This play will work!"

As it turned out, the Trojans needed no special plays. All they needed were three touchdowns from Herschel (on runs of 57, 33, and 3 yards) and his season-high total for one game: 238 yards on 28 carries. They also put up a stubborn defense, never letting Savannah Country Day inside the Johnson County 42-yard line, although Savannah cooperated generously by turning over the ball four times on interceptions and twice on fumbles.

Johnson County won the Region 3-A title easily, 20–0. "Walker is a fine back," the Savannah coach,

Bill Saunders, said in perhaps the night's biggest understatement. "Simply put, we didn't have a very good night and they whipped us."

Even in victory, it wasn't an altogether happy night for the Trojans, either. They lost two players from the starting lineup because of injuries. They wouldn't be available for the state Class A quarterfinal game.

It was a bad omen for Johnson County. The Trojans traveled to within a few miles of the Florida line and lost to the Charlton County team, which had rested for three weeks. Final score: 35–18.

Johnson County finished with a 9-4 record, and the folks who hung out at Bobby·Newsome's Ford and Millers Restaurant were breathlessly counting the days until September 1979. Herschel Walker would be back—bigger, mightier, and faster than ever.

# 5

# "HULK"

If you asked him, Herschel Walker would say his favorite spectator sport is basketball. He also played varsity basketball at Johnson County High as early as his sophomore year. He was no superstar, but he played well enough to be a starting forward.

Even at only 6-foot-1, Herschel was an excellent rebounder. His timing and spring were so good that his teammates nicknamed him "Skywalker," a name taken partly from Luke Skywalker in the movie *Star Wars*. Herschel could jump $40\frac{1}{2}$ inches vertically—from a standing takeoff, not on the run. Which was remarkable, considering that Herschel weighed more than 200 pounds.

As one observer noted, "You're inclined to look at him and say, 'This guy's too musclebound.' But he was an excellent [basketball] player—with a great touch on the ball."

Herschel's favorite sport? Track and field. "I started playing football in the ninth grade," he said, "but I've

**Herschel (25) was a starting forward on the Trojans' basketball team and, though only 6-foot-1, he could stuff the ball.**

been running all my life. I like competition on a one-on-one basis. I enjoy both, but if I had to pick, I'd go one-on-one."

Herschel first developed his sprinter's speed and leg drive by running again and again up the slight incline of the driveway at home. "I wish I had a dollar," his mother said, "for every time Herschel ran up that hill."

For track competition, Herschel worked long, punishing hours on improving his getaway from the starting blocks. Tom Jordan helped him strengthen his legs and hip power by rigging up a mud-grip truck tire (with a 16-pound shot inside) to a 15-foot steel cable that was attached to a leather belt fastened around Herschel's waist. Herschel pulled the tire 20 yards, and sometimes 40 and 60 yards. As his buddy Milt Moorman recalled, "He used to drag me over to the track on Sunday afternoon, our one day off, and we'd pull the tire till I couldn't pull it no more. But Herschel, he'd be pulling on it till it got dark."

The hard work paid off. Herschel led Johnson County to the state Class A track and field championship in the spring of 1979. In the process, Herschel won three events—the 100- and 220-yard dashes and the shot put. He also was the anchor man (the final runner) on the winning mile relay team and second-place 440-yard relay team. Herschel's sprint times in the state meet were 9.8 and 21.8 seconds (the latter tying a state record).

His spectacular showing in the state track meet earned Herschel a trip to New York during the summer of 1979.

Herschel represented Georgia at the Hertz Number 1 Award ceremonies honoring the outstanding high school track and field athlete from each of the 50 states.

Willis and Christine Walker didn't want Herschel to visit New York by himself. So Gary Phillips and Tom Jordan and their wives accompanied Herschel.

Meanwhile, even though Herschel seldom lifted weights, he muscled up to 218 pounds, 13 more than his playing weight as a junior. He stuck to his everyday routine of pushups, situps, and wind sprints.

By the fall of 1979, the start of Herschel's senior year, friends called him "Hulk" (as in the TV show *The Incredible Hulk*). His physique bulged with so many rippling muscles that his mother had to buy extra fabric and reshape his three-piece suits so they fit. Herschel was now about as powerfully built as he would be in college. A writer, Terry Todd, would describe Herschel's upper body in a *Sports Illustrated* article as looking "rather like a dark brown, triangularly shaped nylon sack filled with just the right number of 16-pound shots."

When the high school scraped up enough money to buy weights, many wondered: how many pounds could Herschel lift? "I'd hoped to use 250 pounds as a sort of goal for all the bigger players on the team,"

Phillips said, "but I remember watching in amazement that first day as Herschel took that 250-pound barbell and pumped it up and down,' up and down, like it was made of Styrofoam. After he was finished, he looked over at me, genuinely puzzled, and said, 'Coach, 250 ain't heavy.' "

The college recruiters had begun to hear of Herschel during his junior year in 1978. Now, all during the 1979 football season and into the early spring of 1980, they poured into Wrightsville to watch Herschel run. Rumors and distractions swirled relentlessly around Herschel and his teammates. The Walkers lost some of their privacy. Willis Walker disgustedly ripped out the telephone line. Then the Walkers reordered phone service, with an unlisted number.

During the fall of 1979 Herschel visited Tom Jordan almost every afternoon at the grade school where Jordan taught gym classes, before Johnson County's football workouts. "We had a set of weights at the elementary school," Jordan said. "Herschel would come over to work out with them. It didn't take too long for people to figure out he was comin' over there. . . . Sometimes the crowds at the grade school looked like a Who's Who of college coaches."

Whenever Herschel escaped from the crowds, he quietly sounded out those whose opinions he valued. Jordan recalled one particular occasion, when Herschel asked him: "Coach, if you were me, where would you go to school?"

"I told him, 'Herschel, I know where I would go, but I don't know where you want to go,' " Jordan said. "And then we sat down and talked about different schools. I never told him where I thought he should go. I told him, 'Shoot, boy, you made higher scores on the college board exams than I did. You oughta be able to figure out what you want to do.' He never wanted anybody to make a decision for him. He would like for you to suggest things, and give him several options, and let him decide from there."

Through all those months in 1979 and 1980 Herschel remained calm. He got help from Phillips and Jordan, who screened contacts, weeded out phonies, and tried to keep Herschel's life as undisturbed as possible. They sized up the promises and, if asked, offered advice. They acted as consultants when Herschel and his parents sat down with recruiters who visited the Walkers' home. Herschel's coaches also helped ease the frenzy of perhaps America's hottest recruiting competition since UCLA lured 7-foot-1$^3/_8$ Lew Alcindor (now Kareem Abdul-Jabbar) from New York to play basketball two decades earlier.

Phillips said he told Herschel: "I'm going to make this as good as I can, if you'll let me. I'll shield you from everything, if you want me to. All you have to do is be a kid. You be a high school senior, and you enjoy it. Let this be the happiest year of your life."

"Fine," Herschel replied. "Whatever you want to do."

When the 1979 football season started, thousands of pairs of eyes all over Georgia were on Herschel. In the opening game against West Laurens, Al Rowland, a small reserve fullback, was the star with two touchdowns, but Herschel didn't disappoint anybody. He brought the crowd to its feet in the second quarter when he broke away for a 65-yard touchdown run. He ran the ball only 13 times and finished with 137 yards as Johnson County won, 32–13.

Herschel's kid brother, Lorenza, a sophomore defensive end, got Johnson County's scoring machine rolling the following week when he tackled a Wilkinson County player for a safety in the first quarter. Herschel took over from there, scoring two touchdowns in a 37–6 victory.

Still, Gary Phillips was unhappy with team penalties, and he felt that Herschel wasn't running with his usual authority.

"We talked to him about his style," Phillips said. "He looked different than he did the year before. We thought he jitterbugged too much, instead of hitting the holes right away."

In the next game, Herschel ran with reckless abandon. He scored five touchdowns against East Laurens (on runs of 2, 49, 20, 5, and 69 yards) and amassed 208 yards before Phillips removed him early in the

The pregame buildup inspired Herschel (far left), who took the driver's seat and raced 96 yards for a touchdown as the Trojans ran over the Metter High Tigers.

third quarter. Johnson County won, 47–7, and Herschel told a reporter that it was probabaly his best game ever. "I couldn't believe it when Coach told me I had 208 yards in the third quarter," Herschel said. "When things are going that good, you don't get tired."

Against Metter, Herschel clashed head-to-head with fullback-linebacker Robert Horton, who was an outstanding college prospect and would one day play for Georgia Tech.

For a while Metter's home crowd sensed that an upset was possible. Trailing only 7–0 in the second quarter, Metter punted Johnson County deep into a hole, back on the 4-yard line.

But the Trojans crawled out of it in a hurry. They called the "blast" play—and Herschel did exactly that. He shot through the middle so quickly that nobody even touched him. He scooted 96 yards, the longest scoring run of his high school career. He was so far in front of everybody that he walked across the goal line.

It was the second touchdown of the night for Herschel, who finished with 155 yards on 20 carries. Johnson County stayed unbeaten, 19–6, but not until Robert Horton had gotten in some vicious licks against Herschel. As Phillips remembers, "Horton is the only guy I ever saw hit Herschel in the open field, one on one, and knock him down. Not really tackle him, but hit him—bang!"

It rained the following week in Cochran, Georgia, where Herschel & Company met Bleckley County, a team they'd never beaten. The field was a quagmire, with shoetop-deep puddles in some places. Johnson County led only 7–0 at halftime, after Herschel had sloshed over from one yard out.

At halftime Johnson County's team chaplain, the Reverend Harold Burrell, was said to have listened to a radio interview with the Bleckley County coach. "Here comes Harold, our trusted preacher, telling us that their coach had sorta downplayed Herschel on the radio," Phillips said. "I'm sure Harold probably exaggerated. . . . Well, we really used that to our advantage. We challenged Herschel with it."

And Herschel responded. Suddenly he stood in front of his teammates and said, "I want to tell everybody that I haven't played very well this half. But I'm gonna show that coach what a good back is all about!"

The preacher's story worked. Herschel and his teammates went on to trample Bleckley County, 28–7. Along the way, Herschel scored three more touchdowns and finished with 254 yards. On one play Herschel rambled 45 yards to a touchdown, but it was wiped out by a 15-yard penalty. No problem. On the very next play Herschel scored again—this time from 60 yards out!

Outside Johnson County's locker room afterward, assistant coach Mike Cavan of Georgia and head coach Danny Ford of Clemson waited to say hello to Herschel. So did another recruiter named Norm Van Brocklin. He was a pro football Hall of Fame quarterback who had led the Los Angeles Rams to the National Football League championship in 1951 and the Philadelphia Eagles to the NFL's 1960 title—15 months before Herschel was born. Later, he would coach the Minnesota Vikings and the Atlanta Falcons.

When Herschel emerged from the locker room, Van Brocklin introduced himself. Then Herschel boarded the bus with his teammates for the ride back to Wrightsville.

"Coach," Herschel asked Gary Phillips, "who was that man?"

"Herschel," Phillips replied with surprise, "that was Norm Van Brocklin. He was a great pro player!"

"Oh," Herschel said. "I never heard of him."

# 6

# THE DREAM SEASON

The noise outside was loud enough to disturb the students in Marie Duggan's third-period family living class.

Dust swirled up from the baseball field, and one student, Marcus Hood, scurried to the window to see what all the commotion was about. He looked up in the sky. His eyes widened. Then he screamed, "Mrs. Duggan, Mrs. Duggan, there's a helicopter out there! Mrs. Duggan, it's getting bigger! Mrs. Duggan ... it's *landing!*"

Out of the chopper stepped Pepper Rodgers, the Georgia Tech coach, enjoying all the excitement. He wanted to meet Herschel Walker and give him a nudge about coming to Tech.

Even some politicians wanted Herschel to go to Tech. He received messages from Maynard Jackson, then Atlanta's mayor, and Andrew Young, who would succeed Jackson as mayor. Herschel visited the Tech campus and posed for a picture that caused anxious

51

moments among those who wanted him to go to the University of Georgia, Tech's archrival. The picture showed Herschel standing with Gary Phillips on Tech's home field and beside Tech's "Ramblin' Wreck" jalopy, holding a gold football helmet with Tech's "GT" insignia on it.

But in 1979 Herschel had more pressing business—such as beating Savannah Country Day High School. Practice sessions became rougher than usual. On one play Herschel was tackled with punishing force. He slowly got up, holding his neck. He complained that somebody had illegally grabbed him by the face mask.

"Don't worry about it, Herschel," Phillips said. "We'll come back to that play."

In the huddle, anger blazed in Herschel's eyes. He looked at Phillips and the other players. "Let's run that play again," he said. "Right now!"

"Aw, c'mon, Herschel," Phillips said. "Just forget about it. It's no big deal."

"I said, 'Run the play right now!' " Herschel shot back.

"Okay, gang," Phillips said, "let's give Herschel the ball."

Now Herschel slammed into the middle again. This time he kept his footing. He plowed over the first wave of tacklers and burst into daylight. He ran a zigzag course.

"I mean, Herschel tried to hit as many people as

he could," Phillips said. "Some guys on the sidelines were sort of laughing at the other guys getting mashed. He just ran over there and smashed into one of those guys too. One guy must have thought a truck had run over him."

Phillips noted that it was one of the few times he ever saw Herschel get mad. "Most of the time," he said, "he never really showed much emotion at all."

Herschel had made his point. He made 18 more when he scored three touchdowns (and gained 178 yards) against Savannah Country Day. Johnson County won easily, 25–0, and ran its record to 6-0. But Herschel's team paid a price. Two Johnson County players had been forced out of the game with injuries. Three more players, all starters, were hurt in practice the following week. The Johnson County Trojans went limping into Twin City to play Emanuel County Institute in a battle of unbeatens.

It turned out to be Johnson County's toughest game yet. The injuries took their toll, as did 51 yards in penalties. E.C.I.'s defenders ganged up on Herschel about as well as anybody could. They held him to 102 yards on 24 carries. All the other Johnson County backs could run up only a combined minus 2 yards for the night.

In the end E.C.I.'s Kenny Youmans lined up for a field-goal attempt from 26 yards out. The clock showed only ten seconds left and neither team had scored. The snap was good, and so was the hold.

53

Youmans swung one leg forward and booted the ball skyward.

From his linebacker position, Herschel leaped high in a desperate, last-ditch try to block the kick. But the ball soared over Herschel's outstretched fingertips and through the uprights. E.C.I. won, 3–0, and Johnson County was now a loser for the first time all season.

Afterward, coach Vince Dooley of Georgia consoled Gary Phillips with words to the effect that defeat can build winners. Of course, Dooley knew about losing. His own Georgia team was struggling through an unusually bad season and would finish 1979 with a 6-5 record.

In middle Georgia high school play, meanwhile, the season pretty much came down to Johnson County and E.C.I. Both teams won their next two games. Herschel and his teammates sputtered for nearly three quarters of their homecoming game against Metter. Trailing 12–0, they stormed back on Herschel's three touchdowns (one a diving, fingertip catch of Charles Culver's 20-yard pass) and 179 yards on a school-record 36 carries. Johnson County won, 21–12.

One week later Herschel & Company traveled in style—in a Trailways bus chartered by the Johnson County Booster Club—to their game at Savannah Country Day. They won, 31–8, as Herschel scored all four touchdowns (on runs of 25, 47, 1, and 28 yards) and wound up with 310 yards, a Johnson County High single-game record.

During the game a TV cameraman scampered up and down the field, trying to focus on Herschel. The Savannah coach, Bill Saunders, told the cameraman: "Just stand near the end zone and wait. Herschel's gonna be down there sooner or later."

Everybody was healthy again for Johnson County's rematch with E.C.I., the state's number 1-ranking Class A team. In practice all week Gary Phillips and Tom Jordan sharpened Johnson County's defense by scrimmaging against Herschel. "If we could tackle Herschel, we could tackle anybody," Phillips said.

One Johnson County defender, Thomas Jenkins, was particularly effective against Herschel, even though he weighed only 138 pounds. Jenkins' technique: hit Herschel's shins and knock him off his feet. But even then, Jenkins got up from one frightening collision with Herschel and sighed: "Man, that boy hurts."

The E.C.I. Bulldogs were the only team all season that had kept Herschel from scoring and had defeated Johnson County's Trojans. Well, Herschel & Company hadn't forgotten.

Herschel put on a magnificent show for the home-town fans (and a band of recruiters) in the overflow crowd of 5,000 at Herschel Lovett Stadium. He scored his twenty-seventh, twenty-eighth, twenty-ninth, and thirtieth touchdowns of the year as Johnson

County wrecked E.C.I.'s dream of a perfect season, 32–7. Herschel finished with 237 yards for the game, boosting his season total beyond 2,000 yards.

When it was over, one E.C.I. fan slowly shook his head and said of Herschel: "He looks like a grown man out there, playing against those boys."

Meanwhile, the recruitment of Herschel Walker intensified. Herschel made campus visits to Georgia, Alabama, and Clemson, among other colleges. Recruiters from schools as far away as Nebraska, USC, and UCLA made trips to Wrightsville.

Day after day, college coaches followed Herschel almost everywhere. Callers from across the country telephoned Gary Phillips and Tom Jordan at all hours of the night. Where would Herschel go?

On the week of the regional playoff opener, Herschel caught the flu. It wasn't severe enough, however, to keep him out of the Treutlen County game at Soperton. Johnson County didn't really need him, anyway. The Trojans won, 49–0, even though Herschel played only about half the game. He rushed for 145 yards on 16 carries, scored two touchdowns, and made two interceptions.

Now came the battle everybody had been waiting for—Johnson County vs. Emanuel County Institute, for the third time. At stake was the Region 3-A title. Each team had beaten the other once.

When they arrived in Twin City, Herscheland his teammates needed a police escort through the mobs of E.C.I. fans. The game itself was breathtaking. Both teams moved the ball for huge chunks of yardage. They traded the lead six times before Herschel scored twice in the final six minutes, from 2 and 15 yards out, for his second and third touchdowns, to put the game away, 32–19.

"For just three deflated dollars," Doug Hall wrote in the Dublin *Courier-Herald*, "some 4,000 fans were treated to one of the most rip-snorting high school football games in many moons."

Gary Phillips agreed. "Lord, if this game had gone on five more minutes, I'd have died," he said. "I feel like *this* was the night we won the state championship."

Actually, Herschel and his teammates needed three more wins to reach their goal.

Before the first of those games, Herschel was presented with a football autographed by all his teammates and inscribed HERSCHEL WALKER 2,000 YARDS. His parents were invited to the presentation.

On that same night, rumors circulated that a set of keys to a new car was inside the football and that the Johnson County Booster Club had bought Herschel the car. Actually, the football contained no car keys, but Herschel did get a $9,000 Pontiac Firebird Trans Am—black with gold trim.

Some people wondered who bought Herschel the car. Willis Walker explained that he had taken out a loan to purchase the car for Herschel as a graduation gift. "They told us people would be trying to influence him by giving him fancy gifts," Willis said. "I said, 'Well, one thing they're not going to say is that somebody bought him a car.' That makes me mad. I work double shifts at night in the cold. My wife works hard. We're not asking anybody for anything. And Herschel wasn't taking anything."

It is against the rules of the National Collegiate Athletic Association for a student to accept gifts from recruiters. An NCAA investigator found nothing illegal about Herschel's new car.

All the gossip about the car was secondary to the task at hand for Herschel and his teammates. They needed a win over Charlton County to stay alive in the state Class A playoffs. They got it, 21–0, against the team that had knocked them out of the playoffs the year before. Herschel scored all three touchdowns, rushed for 199 yards, and made 11 tackles.

"Two to go! Two to go!" Johnson County's fans chanted.

Two days later Herschel complained of stiffness in his right shoulder. He had suffered a deep bruise in the Charlton County game. He practiced lightly without pads all week. The rest apparently helped. He ran 50, 69, and 38 yards for all three Johnson County touchdowns in a 21–0 win over Mt. de Sales, a private school from Macon. Herschel also gained 270 yards and crept ever closer to 3,000 for the season.

Now Johnson County played Feldwood High of

College Park, near Atlanta, for the Class A title. Like Herschel, Rex Willis of Feldwood had also exceeded 2,000 yards. But Rex had more than football on his mind: his family's house had burned to the ground the week before the game.

The shops in Wrightsville shut down early. The game had been moved to Saturday night, from Friday, because Feldwood had to travel 160 miles from Atlanta. The crowds arrived at Herschel Lovett Stadium as early as 4 P.M., four hours before the kickoff.

All week long Gary Phillips and Tom Jordan had studied game films of Feldwood, which was unbeaten and once-tied in 12 games. Their preparation would pay off. Feldwood wasn't the kind of team that would roll over dead, not even after Herschel had dashed 65 yards to a touchdown on the game's fourth play. It was all Herschel and his teammates could do to come away tied, 14–14, at the half.

From there, however, things pretty much belonged to Johnson County. The Trojans mounted a third-quarter scoring drive, Herschel plunging over from the 1-yard line to make it 21–17. Linebacker Thomas Jenkins scooped up a Feldwood fumble and raced 92 yards to a touchdown that broke the game open, 28–17. It was all over.

Herschel added his fourth touchdown of the game— and his forty-fifth of the year—on a slanting, twisting 9-yard run through heavy traffic. Final score: 35–17.

The Trojans had run away with the Class A championship, winning 14 of 15 games in a season that youngsters' dreams are made of. In the excitement, Herschel showed some emotion for a change. He jabbed an index finger into the air to signify who was number 1, and his face brightened into a winning smile.

After the game, Herschel and his teammates—and their parents—gave Feldwood's Rex Willis $200 to help the Willis family recover from the fire that had gutted their home.

Outside the locker room, Herschel saw familiar faces: Vince Dooley of Georgia, Danny Ford of Clemson, and recruiters from Florida State and North Carolina State, among other schools.

Soon Herschel would tell reporters that he wished it weren't over. He had finished the year with 3,167 yards and 45 touchdowns, averaging an amazing 8.5 yards each time he carried the ball. His career totals: 6,137 yards and 86 touchdowns, both national high school records. As a linebacker, Herschel also had the team's highest number of tackles.

"We were all one big family and we stayed together," Herschel said. "Our dreams came true. . . . I love each of the coaches just like a father, and they have treated me like a son."

# 7

# HOT DAWG!

The University of Southern California sits in the shadow of the Los Angeles Coliseum, the scene of the 1984 Olympic Games. The school is almost 3,000 miles away from Wrightsville, Georgia, but it made no secret about how badly it wanted Herschel Walker to play for its football team.

Recruiters from USC hoped Herschel might carry on the tradition of outstanding Trojan tailbacks. Four USC tailbacks have won the Heisman Trophy: Mike Garrett, O.J. Simpson, Charles White, and Marcus Allen.

When Herschel visited the USC campus (as well as that of archrival UCLA) during his senior year of high school in 1979, USC had Marcus Allen, who was then a highly regarded freshman fullback.

Allen was being groomed to take over the tailback job from Charles White, the 1979 Heisman Trophy winner and a senior. Herschel and his mother later saw White lead USC over Ohio State, 17–16, in the 1980 Rose Bowl game.

That meant Herschel would have strong competition for the tailback job. And besides, Herschel's mother wasn't enthusiastic about the prospect of her son going to college on the West Coast. Gary Phillips remembers that Christine Walker told Herschel: "California is three thousand miles away. If you get hurt, or they do you wrong out there, there's no telling what could happen before I could get to you to help you."

By the winter of 1980 Herschel still had everybody guessing. Two University of Georgia boosters, Ralph Jackson and Bobby Newsome, both of Wrightsville, were determined not to let Herschel slip away to Clemson, as his cousin William Scott had in 1974. Jackson and Newsome were often seen with Herschel's father at Johnson County High football games. Mike Cavan, a Georgia assistant coach who was assigned to recruit Herschel, made numerous trips to Wrightsville and is said to have often stayed in Newsome's lakeside cabin.

To ease the recruiting pressures on Herschel, Phillips and Jordan consulted with Herschel's parents and established ground rules for college coaches' official "contacts," or visits with Herschel and his family. "No recruiter could come to their house unannounced," Phillips said, "or without the consent of Herschel's parents. We had a couple of instances where people showed up uninvited, and I jumped on them about that."

Of course, Herschel was also busy playing basketball again for the Johnson County High varsity. As a senior, Herschel missed three games because of recruiting trips, but he averaged 12.5 points a game.

Herschel scored 29 points against Bryan County High in a regional basketball tournament semifinal game that propelled Johnson County into the state playoffs. But the Trojans lost to Broxton County High by three points and finished with an 18–9 record (compared with 16–8 the year before).

Just about everywhere he went, Herschel Walker attracted crowds. Recruiters flocked to basketball practice sessions "like crows sitting on telephone wires," Gary Phillips said. Reporters hounded Herschel with postgame questions: "Have you decided yet?" and "When can we expect a decision?"

Christine worried about Herschel. She looked into his eyes, she said, and "they were getting deep in his head. His face was getting long. I said, 'Herschel, I want you to decide to go *somewhere*. Either that, or just decide to stay *home* and say you're not going anywhere.' "

On the first day of spring Herschel told Phillips and Jordan that he had narrowed his choices (from more than a hundred scholarship offers) to three schools—Georgia, Clemson, and Georgia Tech.

At 5:00 A.M. on Easter Sunday, April 6, Christine Walker was awakened by a noise. She whispered to Willis: "It's Herschel. I don't know what's bothering him. He's gone outside."

Christine got up and walked to the front of the house. Peering into the semidarkness outside, she saw Herschel jog down the long dirt driveway, where he'd sprinted umpteen hundred times against Veronica. "I thought to myself, 'Herschel goin' jogging *this* early in the morning?' " Christine said. "I started fixing breakfast."

A while later, Herschel came back into the house. "Herschel, what's wrong?" his mother asked.

"I think I've made up my mind today," Herschel said.

"You have?"

"Yeah."

"What school are you gonna go to?"

Herschel said nothing. He prolonged the suspense, his mother said, by cutting up scraps of paper. He then asked her to write one of these names on each scrap of paper: Georgia . . . Clemson . . . USC . . . Alabama.

Then, she said, Herschel dropped them into a paper bag and shook them up. She laughs warmly now as she tells the story. "I said, 'The first one you pick three times, that's the school you go to.' The first one he pulled out, I think, was Clemson. Then it was

Georgia or Alabama. The last one he picked was USC. . . . But he picked Georgia more times than any of the other three."

Christine then suggested flipping a coin. "If the coin turned up on heads," she said, "that would be the lucky school. Heads might be Georgia; tails might be Clemson. So we did that—and every time it came out Georgia!"

When Christine resumed preparing breakfast, Herschel said, "Mama, I think I'm going to sign today."

"You can't sign today," Christine said, "because today is Sunday."

"Yes, I can. I'm going to sign today. I want you to call coach Jordan."

"You want me to call coach Jordan? Coach Phillips is the head coach. If you want to talk about signing or anything, you ought to talk to coach Phillips."

"You can call him, too, but I want to talk to coach Jordan."

Christine telephoned Gary Phillips and Tom Jordan, informing them that Herschel wanted to see them.

"Herschel has made his decision," she told Phillips.

"Do you mind if I ask you?" Phillips said. "What school is he going to?"

"Georgia," she said.

Phillips then notified Mike Cavan, Georgia's assistant coach, at a relative's home, where Cavan and his family were having an Easter-egg hunt. When Cavan heard the news, he let out a wild, delirious scream.

# 8

# THE FRESHMAN

There was joy in Wrightsville. Mighty Herschel would dress out in Georgia red and black come September. To fans of the University of Georgia, this was exciting news.

But first Herschel had still another world to conquer—the state track and field meet. He led Johnson County to the state Class A title for the second year in a row.

Again Herschel won the 100- and the 220-yard dashes and the shot put. He was also the anchor man on the Trojans' defending champion mile-relay team that raced to a runner-up finish. The 440-yard relay team didn't make it to the state meet. One of Herschel's teammates dropped the baton during the regional meet.

Herschel's fastest time in the 100-yard dash during his senior year in 1980 was 9.7 seconds, two-tenths of a second slower than what he ran as a junior. Gary Phillips, looking back on Herschel's high school career, said he never saw any athlete so young excel so much with such a minimum of excess energy. "He's got economy of effort, which is probably what makes him such a great athlete," Phillips said. "He knows exactly when to turn the motor on and off, and when to idle. All great athletes have that ability. It's just a natural thing. You can't teach that. He ran as hard as he had to—and he'd run a 9.7. If he had to give it a little bit more to win, he'd run 9.5."

Herschel excelled in his studies, too. He graduated first in his class of 108 pupils at Johnson County High. He had a grade average of 93 and he was elected by his classmates to serve as president of the Beta Club, a scholastic honor society. "On Friday nights, when the other kids were out chasing, he'd be over at my house, playing Yahtzee," Tom Jordan said. "His mental discipline was incredible."

Gary Phillips said of Herschel: "He always seemed, to me, to be a little bit older than his peers. And a lot more mature. I thought he was a couple of years ahead of his class, in terms of maturity, both physically and mentally."

During the summer of 1980, Herschel played in the North vs. South state high school football game in Atlanta. His South team was trounced, 34–7, and he carried the ball 13 times for only 55 yards. "I think I did fair, but I didn't play up to my potential," he said.

It was August 1980 and soon Herschel would say

good-bye to Wrightsville. He wrote a poem entitled "It's Almost Gone":

> It's time to move on
> And give life a try . . .

On his last day of summer vacation, Herschel said farewell to his family and his buddy Chris Troup. Then he drove to Herschel Lovett Stadium, which sat empty in the hot August sun, but was filled with memories of his long touchdown runs.

The next morning Herschel awoke before dawn. He quietly left his room. Taped to one wall was his sketch of Martin Luther King, Jr., flanked by drawings of John and Robert Kennedy. He loaded up his Trans Am with clothes and other belongings. His destination was Athens, Georgia.

He didn't wake his family. He drove away, into the sunrise.

Ninety-four miles away Herschel reached Athens, home of the University of Georgia, one of the oldest institutions of higher learning in America. The university, which was chartered in 1785, did not accept black students until 1961. Its varsity football team did not have a black player until 1972.

In a setting of red-brick, white-pillared buildings and sheltering live oaks, Herschel reported for football practice. On the first day of contact drills he took a handoff and rocketed into the line. Right there to meet him was a junior nose guard with "M. WEAVER" on his helmet. At 6 feet and 270 pounds, Eddie (Meat Cleaver) Weaver had almost the physique of a Sumo wrestler.

Wham! A terrifying collision. Herschel crash-landed in a heap. When the pileup untangled, Herschel rose slowly. Welcome, Herschel, to the Southeastern Conference.

On Herschel's second carry he bashed into Weaver again, but spun off him and lunged forward. The third time he fumbled. Thereafter, he slid through holes and found daylight.

A reporter asked Herschel, "Have you ever been hit harder than on that first time against Eddie Weaver?"

"No, sir," Herschel said, "I don't think so. He got me up high, right under the shoulder pads."

"Were they hitting you so hard because your name is Herschel Walker?"

"No, sir. I think they were hitting everybody pretty hard. . . . I was jittery a little bit at first. But after that first hit, I was okay. I think that first lick got me into college football."

Herschel was only the third-string tailback when the Georgia Bulldogs went to Knoxville, Tennessee, to play their 1980 season opener against the Tennessee Vols.

It was a muggy, 90-degree Saturday night in early September. A crowd of 95,288—the largest ever to see a football game in the South—crammed into newly expanded Neyland Stadium.

Herschel, a freshman clad in Georgia jersey number 34 (he'd asked for 43, his high school numeral, but it had been claimed by an upperclassman), knew he was a long way from Wrightsville. He looked up, up, up at the towering decks of Neyland Stadium and felt, as he put it later, "paralyzed . . . I felt I was falling apart."

Vince Dooley, Georgia's coach, had brought Herschel along slowly in preseason practice, sensing that Herschel was under enough pressure already from enormous preseason publicity.

Georgia fell behind early, 9–0. Its attack was stifled by missed blocks, fumbles, delay-of-game penalties, and a veteran Tennessee defense that plugged up the holes with speed. Donnie McMickens, the starting tailback, was stopped. So was Carnie Norris, his replacement, except for one 16-yard run.

Meanwhile, at home five miles outside of Wrightsville, the Walker family was getting poor radio reception on the broadcast of the game. The static wouldn't go away, so Willis Walker parked the family car up close to the front porch and turned on the car radio. It worked!

In Knoxville, Vince Dooley was unhappy with Georgia's play. It was the second quarter. "Herschel!" he yelled. "Get in there!"

Back in Wrightsville, Herschel's brothers and sisters began to jump up and down. "Do it, Bo!" they screamed.

On his very first college run Herschel gained two yards. Then he powered for six yards. The crowd perked up. Soon he flared out of the backfield and reached high to grab a nine-yard pass from Buck Belue. He would later say that he got hit "a real good lick" on the play. "I came out of it," he said. "I felt good after that."

Now Tennessee's quarterback, Jeff Olszewski, hurled a 36-yard touchdown pass to widen the Vols' lead to 15–0 late in the third quarter. Georgia soon recovered a fumbled Jim Broadway punt in the end zone for a safety, making the score 15–2.

That seemed to give the Dawgs a new lease on life. Driving from midfield, they reached the Tennessee 16-yard line. There, Herschel's number was called again—this time on a play called a pitch sweep.

Herschel took the pitchout from Buck Belue and cut into traffic. Lowering his head, he bowled over Mike Casteel, a 216-pound defensive end. Now Herschel burst into the clear, but he soon ran into more traffic at the 10-yard line. There, he slammed head-on into safetyman Bill Bates, toppling him like a bowling tenpin. Then Herschel blasted through two more Tennessee defenders at the 5. Touchdown!

In Wrightsville, Herschel's sisters and brothers cheered excitedly. Willis Walker lay on the ground, tears of joy in his eyes.

72

When asked later why he didn't try to run around Bates, Herschel replied, "The shortest distance between two points is a straight line."

Now it was 15–9, and Tennessee lost a fumble at its 37-yard line. Georgia took the ball from there to the Tennessee 9, where Herschel worked his magic again.

This time Herschel picked up an escort of blockers and swept around end. It was easier this time. Touchdown again! Rex Robinson kicked his second extra point of the night, and Georgia held on for the final 11 minutes to win, 16–15. Herschel finished with 84 yards on 24 carries—a splendid debut for an 18-year-old freshman.

Tennessee head coach Johnny Majors had been the coach at Pittsburgh when Tony Dorsett, the 1976 Heisman Trophy winner, set the all-time rushing record for a college football career. Majors was impressed with Herschel. "It looks like Walker will be changing a few defenses as he goes along," he said. "We tried to make some adjustments to stop him, but you can't expect a freshman to have a better start than he did."

Suddenly "How 'Bout Them Dawgs!" bumper stickers sprouted all over Georgia. For Herschel's home debut at Georgia's Sanford Stadium, a crowd of 60,150 turned out to watch Georgia play Texas A & M. Herschel didn't disappoint them. He rushed for 145 yards, including a breakaway 76-yard run—

his third touchdown of the day—as the Dawgs won, 42–0. "I've seen a lot of good running backs," the A & M coach, Tom Wilson, said, "but I don't know if I've ever seen one at that young age as good as that one."

Like O.J. Simpson did in the pros, Herschel praised his blockers. "I just followed my blocks," he said. "Nat Hudson and Jim Blakewood threw some up the middle, and the whole line did—Hugh Nall and Tim Morrison and Jeff Harper . . . Jimmy Womack [the fullback] threw a good one on the linebacker to get me going, and [wide receivers] Amp Arnold and Lindsay Scott threw some real good blocks on the cornerbacks."

The next game was at home against Clemson. Clemson fans—still upset because Herschel chose to go to Georgia instead of Clemson—began to arrive in Athens with bumper stickers that read "Herschel Who?"

The Tigers held Herschel to only 12 yards in the first half, but then he added 109 to finish with 121. The Dawgs won, 20–16.

Next came Texas Christian, and Herschel slid off left tackle, bounced off several defenders, and raced 41 yards to set up Georgia's first touchdown. Herschel left the game with a sprained right ankle and got only 69 yards on nine carries, but Georgia won again, 34–3. "We hit him six times and he kept going,"

TCU's coach, F.A. Dry, commented.

Herschel played only part-time in a 28–21 win over Mississippi because of his tender ankle. Carnie Norris took up the slack, with 150 yards on only 15 carries.

A healthy Herschel returned for the Vanderbilt game, and Georgia fans chanted "HER-schel! HER-schel!" Scoring from 60, 48, and 53 yards out, Herschel finished with a whopping 283 yards on 23 carries—shattering Charley Trippi's single-game Georgia record of 239 yards. Final score: Georgia 41, Vanderbilt 0.

Against South Carolina, Herschel was matched in a nationally televised game against George Rogers, a big strong running back and the leading candidate for the 1980 Heisman Trophy.

The Dawgs had beaten Kentucky, 27–0, the week before and ran their record to 7-0. Now they turned back South Carolina, 13–10, but only after Herschel outgained Rogers, 219 yards to 168. Herschel broke a 76-yard touchdown run, outsprinting three South Carolina defenders who had an angle on him. "He taught me something speeding down that sideline," Rogers said. "He's gonna do a lot. I wasn't nowhere near him as a freshman. And he's got three more years. Amazing."

Next, Herschel burst away on a 72-yard touchdown run in the first quarter against Florida in Jacksonville. But the Dawgs needed a miracle—a 92-yard pass-run play from Belue to Lindsay Scott—to pull the game out, 26–21. Georgia moved to number 1 in the polls.

Herschel gained 77 yards and scored once against Auburn as the Dawgs won again, 31–21. Then came the regular-season finale against Georgia Tech. Herschel needed 41 yards to break Tony Dorsett's one-season NCAA freshman record. He got 205 yards—including three touchdowns from 65 and 23 yards out and a 1-yard plunge. That gave Herschel a record 1,616 yards for the season as the Dawgs wrecked Tech, 38–20.

Next stop: the Sugar Bowl game in New Orleans.

There, on January 1, 1981, Herschel and the Dawgs created a perfect ending to a perfect season. Despite a painful left shoulder that had popped out of its socket, Herschel rushed for 150 yards on 36 carries and scored both touchdowns as Georgia won its first national championship ever, 17–10.

"He's greater in person than on film," Notre Dame's retiring coach, Dan Devine, said.

Linebacker Bob Crable of the Irish agreed. "His legs are so strong," he said, "you can't hit him and knock him down."

Herschel didn't win the Heisman Trophy, which goes annually to college football's top player (that honor went to George Rogers), but he was the first freshman consensus All-American in this century.

In the excitement outside the locker room, red-clad Georgia fans toasted Herschel and got ready to paint the town red.

Nearby stood another Georgian, President Jimmy Carter, and his wife, Rosalynn. The President asked Herschel to pose with him and the First Lady—and Herschel happily obliged.

# 9

# "I'VE SHOWN HOW
# I CAN PLAY"

His first name alone sprang up all across Georgia. It was seen on bumper stickers in Athens ("See My Cousin Herschel Run"), on hats in Americus, on T-shirts in Augusta, on posters in Atlanta. And, as far away as New York's Belmont Park, a two-year-old thoroughbred won its debut in track-record time. The colt's name: "Herschelwalker."

On the football field Herschel won praise across the land. Vince Dooley said Herschel must have come from "another planet." The Dallas Cowboys' super-scout, Gil Brandt, declared that only Herschel and Earl Campbell were good enough fresh out of high school to play in the NFL. And quarterback Buck Belue put it simply: "I may be handing off to the best that's ever played."

Off the field Herschel politely autographed little boys' sneakers and grown men's souvenir programs. He gave motivational talks on videotape—about the

Herschel soared as if, in his coach's words, he came from another planet.

need to stay in school—to Atlanta-area high school students. He didn't growl at reporters who asked stupid questions, even if he'd heard them for the zillionth time. He didn't smoke, or blow in his soup, or even sip watered-down booze.

"No alcohol? Not even out of curiosity?" someone asked Herschel.

"I'm curious about jumping off a cliff," Herschel replied, "and I don't do that, either."

And drugs?

"No. My body is a temple that I should keep sacred and clean. You have to deal with problems, and even if you take a million dollars worth of drugs, your problems are still going to be there when the money's gone."

To young and old, black and white, rich and poor, Herschel became, at 19, an authentic American hero. "Somebody like him, you see once in a lifetime," said Georgia teammate Jimmy Payne. "I mean, he's unique. I tell you, if I had children, I'd like them to grow up and be similar to him."

Just about everywhere he went, Herschel created excitement. Crowds swarmed around him at basketball games. Things soon got so out of hand that Herschel couldn't go to the games anymore. Yet for somebody who stirred up so much excitement, he still managed to keep his thoughts to himself. "I don't think too many people can get the real feelings out of me," Herschel said. "People think I'm a strange guy. I'm a deep thinker. My life inside is my private life. I have friends, but no best friend. You can never totally open yourself. Your closest friend can be your baddest enemy. . . ."

At home in Wrightsville, Christine Walker told a visitor that she wished Herschel would "open up. I wish he would have somebody to talk to."

Now even greater pressures would be put on him. Herschel Walker meant big money.

An insurance company wanted to use him to sell insurance, and the Canadian Football League wanted him to leave school and turn pro.

Willis Walker, meanwhile, said Herschel could do whatever he pleased. "If Herschel says, 'I'm gonna stay at Georgia,' I'll be happy," he said. "If Herschel says, 'I'm going to Canada,' I'll be happy. If Herschel wants to haul pulpwood, I'll be happy. People think we influence Herschel. We can't tell that boy nothing. Heck, he's smarter than me in a lot of ways. How can I tell him what to do when I ain't never been through anything like that? That Herschel's got a level head on his shoulders. He'll make the right decision."

Christine Walker, for her part, was more assertive than Willis. She told Herschel flatly that she wanted him to stay in school: "I said to him, 'Herschel, you're just too young. It's a big world out there. People are much older and more experienced. I wish you wouldn't do that.' "

As it turned out, Herschel took his mother's words to heart. On April 30, 1981, Herschel announced that he had decided to stay at Georgia. "I was born in this country," he said, "and it does not seem right to leave the country to play pro football."

At that time, Herschel was running on the Georgia track team. He was excused from spring football practice. He usually ran only a step or two behind such world-class sprinters as Carl Lewis, Stanley Floyd, Allen Wells, and Mel Lattany (now an assistant track coach at Georgia). All Herschel lacked was consistency.

When his Georgia track coach, Lewis Gainey, first scouted him in high school, Herschel appeared out of place—like a bull among cheetahs. "But there was no doubt in my mind he was talented," Gainey said. "It's unique to have a sprinter that big run so fast. Many people say because of his size that he has an awkward running form, but he is a power runner. No one can really say his form is wrong, because he's different from the smaller runner. There haven't been too many athletes his size and strength to compare him to."

In qualifying heats for the 55-meter dash in an indoor meet at the New Jersey Meadowlands, Herschel outsprinted Harvey Glance, once the "world's fastest human," and Houston McTear, who had held the world record in the outdoor 100-yard dash. Herschel finished third in the finals. Later in the same meet, he outran Floyd, the world's premiere sprinter in 1980 and the 60-meter indoor champion. Herschel's fastest 60 meters to date: 6.14 seconds.

Things were pretty much the same at the NCAA indoor championships at Baton Rouge, Louisiana. Herschel surprised many observers by running 10.22 seconds—his best time then in the 100 meters—and finishing second in a semifinal heat. In the finals he placed seventh. Photographers and reporters surrounded him in the infield afterward. Carl Lewis, the winner, watched it all from not far away—by himself.

Outdoors, Herschel ran even better during the spring and summer of 1981. He sprinted the second leg on Georgia's Southeastern Conference (SEC) champion and NCAA runner-up 440-yard relay team, which broke the school record at 39.34 seconds. He outran Carl Lewis, then the NCAA champion and world's fastest sprinter of 1981, in the quarterfinals and semifinals of the 100 meters in a meet at Sacramento, California. Herschel withdrew from the finals because of an injury.

From there, Herschel joined the Athletic Attic Track Club and toured West Germany, Holland, Switzerland, and the Soviet Union for three weeks during the summer. It seemed that the big crowds in Amsterdam—55,000—inspired him. He ran the 100 meters there in 10.19 seconds—his fastest-ever clocking. With that effort, he joined the world's top 20 sprinters.

The trip to Europe was rewarding in other ways too. "It was a good learning experience for me to get into a new culture and to learn new things," he said.

At the start of football practice in 1981, Herschel's parents took out a $1 million insurance policy—from Lloyd's of London—against any injury that might end Herschel's football career.

Said Herschel before the 1981 opening game against Tennessee: "This year I'm bigger, stronger, quicker, and more powerful. I can do almost anything. They haven't seen the Herschel Walker of September 5, 1981; they've seen the one from last year."

Herschel lived up to his words. He slashed and dashed for 161 yards on 30 carries, scoring the game's first touchdown on a 1-yard smash, as the Dawgs blasted Tennessee, 44–0.

Against Clemson, it just wasn't Georgia's—or Herschel's—day. Herschel fumbled three times, losing the ball twice. He gained 111 yards on 28 carries. Buck Belue threw five interceptions and fumbled once. Tight end Norris Brown dropped several passes, including one at the Clemson 3-yard line that had "touchdown" written all over it. In all, the Dawgs lost nine turnovers, and Clemson's roaring, orange-clad fans loved every minute of it. Their beloved Tigers had stopped the nation's longest winning streak at 15 games. Final score: 13–3.

Back home in Athens, Georgia fans noticed that

Herschel had scored only one touchdown so far that season and hadn't run longer than 22 yards on any single play. Many forgot that Georgia had lost four of their five starting linemen—the players who clear the way for the running backs. Again and again, they asked: "What's wrong with Herschel?"

The questions bothered Herschel more than anyone ever knew. Herschel even thought of quitting football the next week—after only three games of his sophomore year. "I dragged through practice halfheartedly. My mind focused more on what I would tell Coach Dooley than how I'd run against South Carolina," Herschel wrote in a 1982 issue of *Guideposts*, a spiritual publication. "I decided it might be easier to just quit, to forget the pressures and the questions, the pain that came when your best effort wasn't good enough. I decided to wait until the next morning to say anything about quitting."

That night, Herschel gazed for a long, long time at an illustration of Christ, mounted on a wall in his room. "I just looked, drawing strength from the picture," he said. "And when I got to thinking again about why I needed the strength, I realized I'd found the example I needed to follow. Whether the criticisms of me had been fair or not, it didn't matter. Herschel Walker would be no quitter, either."

Too bad for South Carolina. The next weekend, at Athens, Herschel rolled up 176 yards—his biggest total yet in the 1981 season—and scored twice from close range. Final score: Georgia 24, South Carolina 0.

Now it was on to Ole Miss. Herschel treated the crowd to his finest running of the season. Despite having a bruised foot, Herschel carried 41 times for 265 yards and a touchdown. As the dying seconds ticked away in Georgia's 37–7 win, the Ole Miss cheering section stood up behind the Dawgs' bench and chanted, "HER-schel! HER-schel! HER-schel!"

The next weekend, the Dawgs traveled to Nashville and picked on lowly Vanderbilt, 53–21. Herschel rushed for 188 yards on 39 carries and scored twice from inside the 5-yard line. His yardage total gave him 2,684 during his Georgia career, breaking Kevin McLee's school record (2,581).

Fighting a heavy cold, Herschel ran for 129 yards on 33 carries and scored from one yard out as the Dawgs returned home and shut out Kentucky, 21–0.

Whatever happened to those long-distance touchdown runs—the kind that Herschel used to make as a freshman? As Georgians waited for Herschel to break one, Herschel dismissed it all as nothing to get worked up about. "Not many backs in the country have had as many ten- to fifteen-yard runs as I have this year," he said. "I just keep sticking my head in there and taking what I can get."

And what about the Heisman Trophy race? USC's Marcus Allen had run well ahead of Herschel in total yardage by midseason. But that didn't seem to perturb Herschel, either. "Jimmy Carter voted for himself as President," he said. "I reckon I would vote for myself. I believe in myself. If I win it, great. If not, hard luck. There have been a lot of super athletes that never won the Heisman Trophy. Walter Payton never won it. Joe Namath never won it."

With Herschel gaining 112 yards and scoring four touchdowns, Georgia trampled Temple, 49–3, and warmed up for its annual showdown with Florida at the Gator Bowl in Jacksonville. A crowd of more than 68,000 jammed the stadium.

Florida got off to a 14–0 lead, but stormed back when Herschel caught touchdown passes of 24 and 16 yards from Buck Belue. Herschel added a 4-yard scoring run. Then he smashed over from the 1 with his fourth touchdown of the game, culminating a 95-yard drive in which the Dawgs frantically raced the clock to pull the game out, 26–21. All told, Herschel carried 47 times (an SEC and Georgia record) for 192 yards.

"He was definitely the difference in the game," Florida coach Charley Pell said.

Auburn didn't have any luck against Herschel, either. He rang up 165 yards—boosting his one-season record beyond the 1,616 yards he had gained the year before—and scored a school-record-tying sixteenth touchdown (shared with Frank Sinkwich). The Dawgs won, 24–13.

Against Georgia Tech the landslide was even worse. Herschel scored four touchdowns and ran for 225 yards, setting an avalanche of records, including an SEC one-season mark of 1,891 yards, as Georgia won, 44–7.

When it was over, Herschel was openly disappointed that he'd finished runner-up to Marcus Allen in the Heisman Trophy balloting. Ironically, Allen, who finished with an NCAA-record 2,342 yards, and Herschel would have competed for the USC tailback job if Herschel had picked the Trojans instead of Georgia when he was in high school.

"Really, I don't know what else I could have done this year," Herschel said. "I reckon maybe I have to gain three thousand yards. I know Marcus Allen had more yards, but I'm sure a lot of times players have won [the Heisman] who finished second or third in the statistics. I think I have proven what I can do with the football. I've shown how I can play."

Now came a return trip to the Sugar Bowl—this time against Pittsburgh. It would be a more versatile Georgia team than the one that beat Notre Dame for the national championship. The Dawgs, besides riding Herschel's power running, relied heavily on their Buck Belue-to-Lindsay Scott passing game.

Going into New Year's Day, 1982, the Dawgs ranked number 2 in the nation behind their only conquerors all year—Clemson. A second national title in a row was within reach.

But it wasn't to be. With the lead changing hands six times, the Dawgs and Pitt battled down to the wire after Herschel scored two of Georgia's three touchdowns and rushed for 94 yards. The crowd of 77,224 in the Superdome was kept in suspense until the final 35 seconds, when Pitt's Dan Marino passed 33 yards to tight end John Brown on fourth down for the game-winning touchdown. Score: Pitt 24, Georgia 20.

Worse yet for the Dawgs, unbeaten Clemson locked up the national championship by defeating Nebraska in the Orange Bowl. Clemson can perhaps thank Herschel for providing some of its own motivation.

During the week of the bowl games, Herschel had said: "If we played Clemson again tomorrow, we'd beat them and really beat them bad."

# 10

# RUNNING FOR THE HEISMAN

For Herschel Walker, life at the University of Georgia was like a marathon run. To maintain his daily schedule, he almost couldn't waste time sleeping.

His classes, during one sophomore term, began at 7:50 A.M. with a physical education course in karate (he's a brown belt). Then came classes in speech, in propaganda and communications, in American literature, and in philosophy.

At noon each day Herschel went to the athletes' cafeteria at McWhorter Hall, where a wall sign read WE GOT TO GET OUR STUFF TOGETHER. He often snacked on a bag of potato chips while teammates sat down to bigger meals. Then it was off to the Georgia sports information department, where he granted interviews to reporters and held press conferences every Tuesday during football season. And then, by 3 P.M., he was on the practice field, running, stretching, scrimmaging, and blasting off tackle, often dishing out as much punishment as he took.

When time permitted, he drove into town in the evening for an hour at the Athens Institute of Karate. He's no Bruce Lee or Chuck Norris, but then, could they run 9.3 and gain 150 yards against Notre Dame? The philosophy of karate, Herschel said, is that it reinforces discipline and control. Obviously, you need those two things, plus stamina, to hit the books and maintain a 3.0 (B) average, to say nothing of writing poetry late at night.

Then came spring of 1982, and Herschel's fancy turned again to track, his first love in sports. Vince Dooley again excused him from spring football practice. "I'm a different person when I run track than when I play football," Herschel told Jackie Crosby, then sports editor of Georgia's student newspaper, the *Red and Black*. "Football is uptight. Track is more relaxed. You see people at meets who give their heart and soul—their best effort every time. That's the kind of people I like to be around, because I don't consider myself a loser. Runners are an elite group. But when you get to know these people, you learn things about them besides racing. There's time to talk to people and find out what they think about things."

Indoors, Herschel had improved his 60-yard dash time from 6.22 seconds the previous year to 6.14 in 1982. Barely out of football pads in January, Herschel hadn't even practiced when he ran in the Olympic Invitational in the New Jersey Meadowlands. He finished third, at 6.23 seconds, in a 55-meter dash won by Stanley Floyd, Houston's world indoor recordholder, in 6.14. A week later, in the Sunkist Invitational in Los Angeles, Floyd won the 50-yard dash in world-record time (5.22 seconds), but Herschel finished third just ahead of the previous recordholder, Houston McTear, in 5.29 seconds, then the world's third-fastest time of 1982. "Now, it's not 'What's that guy doing out here?' " Floyd said. "It's 'How can a man so big run so fast?' "

At the NCAA indoor championships, Herschel placed sixth in the 60-meter dash, thus earning him All-America recognition in track for the second year in a row (the first six finishers in any event qualify for such honors).

Now, with some observers wondering if Herschel would one day become the first consensus four-year All-American in two sports, he entered an outdoor meet, the Spec Towns Invitational, at Georgia. There, Herschel beat his ex-Georgia teammate, Mel Lattany (a member of the 1980 U.S. Olympic team), in the 100-meter finals. Herschel's time: 10.23 seconds.

A painful sciatic nerve in his back bothered Herschel thereafter, and he managed to finish only fourth in the sprints (10.32 and 21.08) at the SEC finals, while anchoring Georgia's 400-meter relay team to second place.

Nevertheless, Herschel clung to his ambitions of making the 1984 Olympics, even though it seemed a longshot. "I wouldn't rule out the possibility that he could make the Olympics," his coach, Lewis Gainey, said in 1982, "but it would be a very difficult task. We're talking about an event where there's less than a second between the first and last finishers in the race. Knowing Herschel's desire and attitude, he can do it. He actually overworks. He doesn't mind hurting."

Hardly anybody noticed, but another Walker also dreamed of the Olympics. Veronica Walker won All-America honors in the NCAA 100-meter dash and the 400-meter relay in 1982. She had finished among the top six in the sprints at the SEC women's championships two years in a row. Her best times: 11.77 and 24.48 seconds. Her coach, Steve Sitler, noted that Veronica excelled in the relays. "She's intimidating," he said, "a lot like her brother."

For Veronica, it never was easy being known only as "Herschel Walker's sister." "When I got here, all I could hear was Herschel this, and Herschel that," she told Earnest Reese of the Atlanta *Constitution*. "I started wondering, 'Well, what about Veronica? I'm a person, too. I'm not just somebody's sister.' "

Apparently not many noticed another young woman track athlete at Georgia, a friend of Veronica's named Cindy DeAngelis. But Herschel had noticed her the year before. Cindy soon fell into the tight inner circle of friends who socialized with Herschel.

Herschel and his sister Veronica had raced as kids and now they practiced together at Georgia, where she had a track scholarship.

Gary Phillips recalls seeing her among the kids who crowded into Herschel's room on football Saturdays during the 1981 season.

When Phillips entered the room, Herschel wrapped an arm around Cindy and said, "Coach, this is my wife!"

Phillips had seen Herschel make jokes before, when Herschel was in high school. Phillips casually said, "Oh, is that right, Herschel?"

"Yeah," Herschel said, with a straight face. "We were married yesterday."

"Is that right?"

Herschel and Cindy looked at each other and broke into laughter. It was a joke after all.

Herschel, meanwhile, looked ahead to playing two more years at Georgia and getting his degree. On March 16, 1982, he called a news conference on the Georgia campus. It was to quiet all the rumors flying around about his turning pro.

The room was crowded with microphones and cameras. He read from a prepared statement: "I have weighed all the facts and have decided I will remain at Georgia and will not challenge the NFL underclassman rule. . . ." The rule he referred to does not allow NFL teams to draft or sign college athletes until they have completed their senior year of college.

"I still feel the rule is basically unconstitutional," Herschel said. "However, I don't want to interfere with the system that's designed to be the best for the majority of people involved. . . . By challenging the rule, I think it could have some detrimental effects, and staying at Georgia will be the best for me in the long run."

During the summer of 1982, Herschel vacationed in Canada. Then he went to New York and joined several other college football players and coaches on the annual NCAA-ABC nationwide preseason promotional tour.

But when the tour reached Atlanta, Herschel complained of headaches and fatigue. He dropped out of the tour before it went on to Dallas, Seattle, and Los Angeles. An Atlanta physician examined Herschel and diagnosed a viral infection and slightly above-normal blood pressure. "He's probably just run down," the doctor said. He ordered Herschel to take a "complete rest" for one week.

"It's been hurting in the back of my head," said Herschel, explaining that he'd suffered from the headaches for about a month. "I guess I've been thinking about practice."

Sunday morning, August 22, 1982. Readers of the Atlanta *Journal-Constitution* awoke to a startling headline across the top of page 1: WALKER BREAKS THUMB, OUT FOR CLEMSON.

In Athens, the news hit like a bombshell. The nationally televised opener with national champion Clemson on Labor Day was only two weeks away.

Could the Dawgs win without Herschel? When would Herschel be healthy enough to play?

"Playing him would be out of the question for at least three weeks because there would be a chance of refracture, even with him wearing a cast," Dr. Mixon Robinson, a partner of Georgia's team orthopedic surgeon, said. "If that happened, it would require another operation, and he'd be out even longer."

The next day Robinson's partner, Dr. William Mulherin, who performed the surgery, said the operation "went real well." But he added, "For Herschel to play against Clemson would be too big a gamble. The thumb could be rebroken and he could be out for the season."

But Herschel suited up for the Clemson game anyway. And he did play briefly. His right thumb in a bulky, protective cast, Herschel entered the game in the second quarter, with the score tied, 7–7. A roar of approval burst from the crowd of 82,122 at Georgia's Sanford Stadium.

At first, Herschel was used as a decoy. He didn't carry the ball until the third quarter, when the Dawgs led, 10–7. He ran hesitantly during a later Georgia drive, and even plunged toward the end zone from the 1-yard line. But an offside penalty killed the play.

The Dawgs settled for a 23-yard field goal by Kevin Butler and fought off a fourth-quarter threat by Clemson to win, 13–7. Herschel carried the ball only 11 times and gained only 20 yards. One of those runs was a twisting, churning 10-yarder.

The Brigham Young game was only five days away, and Herschel felt "a little pinching" from the pins in his thumb during practice. Even so, he played most of the game, still in a cast, and Georgia won it, 17–14, on Kevin Butler's 44-yard field goal with only 1:11 remaining.

Herschel was hardly at 100 percent effectiveness. He fumbled the ball away twice, but gained 124 yards on 31 carries and scored from one yard out to bring the Dawgs to within 14–13. Butler's extra point tied it, 14–14, with $5\frac{1}{2}$ minutes to play.

Six days later the pins were removed from Herschel's thumb, but the cast stayed on. Then, with a week's rest, the Dawgs won at South Carolina, 34–18, behind Herschel's 134 yards and one touchdown (an 11-yard run) and quarterback John Lastinger's two scoring passes to Clarence Kay.

At Mississippi State, a nearly healthy Herschel—his thumb now out of the cast—helped Georgia claw back from behind and then hang on for a 29–22 win that ran the Dawgs' record to 4-0. It was a game that thrust Herschel clearly back into the Heisman Trophy race against such players as quarterback John Elway of Stanford and running back Eric Dickerson of SMU, among others.

"Today, Herschel ran like he did the past two years,"

said George Haffner, the Dawgs' offensive coordinator.

Herschel was said to be completely healed when the Dawgs returned home in mid-October and swamped Mississippi, 33–10. Georgia got 149 yards on 24 carries from Herschel.

That nudged Herschel to yet another record—the SEC mark for most yards in a career. With 4,158 yards, Herschel surpassed the old record of 4,035 by LSU's Charles Alexander, who played between 1975 and 1978. "I had not even considered his record," Herschel said afterward. "I didn't know I was getting close until someone mentioned it to me last week. I'm happy about it, but I'm not a person who jumps around and dances to show my feelings."

The Dawgs struggled most of the way against Vanderbilt, trailing 13–10 after three quarters. But they won going away, 27–13, with Herschel piling up 172 yards on 38 carries and scoring the game's final touchdown on an option pitch from 26 yards out. It was Herschel's longest run yet that season.

Since the Dawgs had won their first six games, the Georgia sports information department mounted its Heisman Trophy campaign for Herschel. Press releases were mailed in envelopes imprinted with a cartoon of a Bulldog mascot holding a sign saying HERSCHEL FOR HEISMAN. AIN'T NOBODY BETTER!

The Dawgs rolled on. Herschel snagged a screen pass from Lastinger for a 64-yard scoring play and picked up 152 yards as Georgia won at Kentucky, 27–14. Then Herschel thrashed Memphis State's defense for 219 yards and two touchdowns in a 34–3 win at home.

Then came the annual border shootout with Florida at Jacksonville. Herschel stormed 10 yards for a touchdown on a power sweep before all the 80,749 fans were in their seats. He scored twice more and amassed 219 yards for the second week in a row. He left the game in the third quarter. Georgia won, 44–0, and Dawg fans chanted, "We're number 1!" Two days later the wire-service polls agreed.

"If Herschel doesn't win the Heisman Trophy," Dooley said, "well—what is the greatest injustice of all time? That would be it."

The following Tuesday, Herschel did receive six votes as a write-in candidate for governor of Georgia. But then, so did E.T. and comic strip characters Pogo and Garfield.

It took a last-gasp, 80-yard scoring drive for the Dawgs to pull out the Auburn game, 19–14, with Herschel blasting over from three yards out for the winning touchdown. That gave the Dawgs their third consecutive Southeastern Conference title. Along the way, Herschel raced 47 yards for Georgia's first touchdown (his longest run in two years) and finished with 177 yards.

Now he could almost taste the Heisman Trophy. "If I haven't shown people in the last two weeks that

I might be worthy of it, I never will," he said. "I'm not going to beg for it. Whether I win it or not, I'll know I deserve it."

In the regular-season finale, Herschel brought Dawg fans at Sanford Stadium to their feet with a sizzling 59-yard touchdown run against Georgia Tech. The game was barely three minutes old. He added a second touchdown, the fifty-ninth of his three-year career. Tech's Robert Lavette outgained Herschel, 203 yards to 167, but the Dawgs overcame a 7–6 halftime deficit and won, 38–18.

The win gave Georgia an 11-0 record and set up a number 1 vs. number 2 showdown on January 1 with once-beaten Penn State. Herschel finished the 1982 season with 1,752 yards, placing him third on the NCAA's all-time career list behind Tony Dorsett and ex-USC tailback Charles White. To overtake Dorsett for the all-time lead, Herschel would need 824 yards in his senior year.

Now a crush of hundreds of Herschel admirers waited outside the Dawgs' dressing room. Crowds surged around him, too, when he strode off the field. They resembled the mobs that swoon over rock musicians or Hollywood idols. As fans thrust souvenir programs in front of him, Herschel muttered, "I'll sign autographs, but I'm gonna keep movin'."

Once he got inside the Georgia Coliseum, where the Dawgs dressed, somebody arranged to sneak Herschel out the back door.

Like secret agents, two student managers waited in a car. When Herschel emerged, one manager yelled, "Quick! Get in the car, Herschel!"

Herschel bounded into the front seat, and the car sped away to the dorm. There, another mob waited. Herschel leaped out and dashed to the dorm as if he were running the Olympic 100 meters. "I'd never seen him have to do that," said Gary Phillips, who had watched from the car. "By now, things were so bad that when you knocked on Herschel's door, somebody would open it a crack. Then you'd barely see somebody's eyes. Most of the time, they weren't Herschel's."

Soon the Heisman votes were tallied, and Herschel's hopes materialized, at long last. It was Herschel in a landslide, far ahead of John Elway, Eric Dickerson, and Michigan flanker Anthony Carter. Herschel became only the seventh junior in history to win the award and the only other Georgia winner besides Frank Sinkwich (1942). The other juniors: Doc Blanchard of Army (1945), Doak Walker of SMU (1948), Vic Janowicz of Ohio State (1950), Roger Staubach of Navy (1963), Archie Griffin of Ohio State (1974), and Billy Sims of Oklahoma (1978).

"This is the greatest thrill of my life because of what the trophy stands for," Herschel said. "Not just an individual, but a team's performance for that season. It is something I will cherish the rest of my life."

Herschel made it clear that he would return to

102

Georgia for the 1983 football season—and another try at the Heisman. (Only Archie Griffin had won the Heisman a second time, in 1975.) "College has helped me be a better person," he said. "I want to continue to grow, so I think I'll continue to attend college."

**His high school coach, Gary Phillips, and wife, Barbara Phillips, were among those who celebrated Herschel's Heisman Trophy at New York's Downtown Athletic Club.**

When Herschel formally received the award at a Downtown Athletic Club dinner in New York, the guests of honor included Herschel's entire family, along with his girlfriend, Cindy DeAngelis.

"This honor I hold real deep in my heart and soul," said Herschel, clad in tuxedo (size 48 long, with a 33-inch waist). "An award like this is not given to one person if he isn't around super people like I have been. It shows that dreams are possible and miracles can happen."

The Walkers, all seated at one table, beamed with pride. Herschel's mother had given him a replica of the trophy the year before—to soothe his disappointment then. The real thing would stay in the Walkers' house in Wrightsville, covered by a large cloth and tucked away in a closet, only to be moved like precious silver to other hiding places every few days to protect it from theft.

# 11

# HERO OR VILLAIN?

It was a quiet Sunday morning in Athens. Quiet—except for the crash of a two-car accident at East Campus Road and Milledge Avenue.

One car overturned, belching smoke. A 67-year-old woman, Jessie Dye, of Watkinsville, Georgia, was trapped inside.

To the rescue came a young man in jogging clothes. He told a neighbor to grab the door handle. Then he jerked the door open, fragments of glass flying all over the ground. He pulled the woman safely out of the wreckage. The hero was Herschel Walker, who then quietly jogged away.

"I couldn't believe how levelheaded Herschel was during the whole thing," the neighbor, Ted Shanks, said. "He stepped right in and took control of the situation."

By the week's end, Herschel had made headlines again—this time in published reports stating that a team called the Chicago Blitz of the newly formed

United States Football League (USFL) had offered Herschel $10 million to sign with them. The offer was reportedly made by George Allen, the team's part owner and head coach.

"I don't think I ever spoke to Mr. Allen," Herschel said. "At least, I haven't been offered any ten million dollars. I don't think many people are being offered ten million dollars to play football. Right now, my attitude is, like I said, my mind is made up. I'm going to come back to Georgia."

The fury of speculation ended hours later when Allen was quoted as saying he was only "kidding." The reports didn't say whom Allen had tried to kid, but they hinted at how the idea might have originated. At a USFL meeting in Tampa, sporting goods manufacturers had unveiled the new league's uniforms. The Chicago Blitz jersey shown was number 34, with the name WALKER across the back.

The next day, Herschel went home to Wrightsville for Herschel Walker Appreciation Day. About 3,000 townspeople and other well-wishers turned out on a bright, chilly December day. There were bands, songs, and a parade for the young man whose name adorned a sign at the courthouse square: CONGRATULATIONS, HERSCHEL.

Georgia's governor, George Busbee, arrived by helicopter and praised Herschel in a speech. Vince Dooley also spoke. So did Christine and Willis Walker, who introduced Herschel's brothers and sisters.

The motorcade traveled from town to the football field at Herschel Lovett Stadium. Herschel's ex-teammates and coaches at Johnson County High rode in a flatbed truck. Ex-fullback Bennie Brantley, now a Wrightsville policeman, was Herschel's bodyguard, already having been his blocker. Another ex-teammate, Ernie Garnto, had returned from Marine duty in Lebanon. Herschel and Cindy rode in a 1957 Thunderbird convertible, waving happily to the crowd.

At the football field, Herschel told the fans: "Life is teamwork. And y'all have been part of my team. If it weren't for you, I wouldn't be anything. I love y'all."

**Wrightsville celebrated Herschel Walker Appreciation Day as Herschel rode in the parade with his girlfriend, Cindy DeAngelis.**

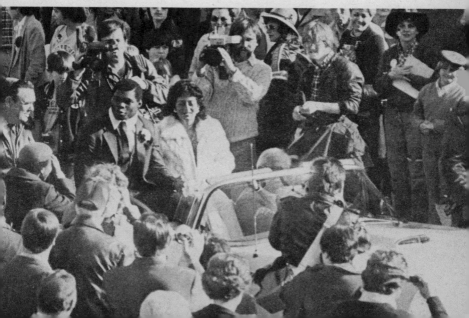

The Wrightsville ceremonies were a time of reflection for Herschel and his proud parents.

Yes, he would stay in school and get his degree, he said. He would play for Georgia in 1983 and take aim at another Heisman and Tony Dorsett's yardage record. And he wanted to run for America in the 1984 Olympics.

Soon to come, however, was the Sugar Bowl game against Penn State, Herschel's and Georgia's third Sugar Bowl in a row.

In New Orleans, the site of the game, anybody who saw Herschel could have understood why the late Elvis Presley couldn't go to the store to buy a loaf of bread. Herschel was mobbed repeatedly by

**Georgia coach Vince Dooley has a word with Herschel at a press conference in New Orleans prior to the Sugar Bowl game against Penn State on January 1, 1983.**

autograph seekers, tourists, camera buffs and, of course, hundreds of red-clad, rebel-yellin' Georgians who shouted, "How 'bout them Dawgs!"

There were press conferences to attend at which Herschel was the center of attention. The reporters wanted to know which team he felt was the favorite.

"If I was a betting man," Herschel said, "I'd put my money on Penn State. They have so many outstanding players and they've played the toughest schedule of any college team. But we have a chance."

Georgia was ranked number 1 and aimed for its second national championship in three years. Penn State was rated number 2, a loss to Alabama smudging an otherwise perfect record. This wasn't as good a Georgia team as the one that had won the title in 1980. But it still had Herschel, the holder of 30 school records, 15 Southeastern Conference records, and 10 NCAA records. Penn State had a great quarterback in Todd Blackledge and a fleet-footed running back in Curt Warner.

What Penn State also had was a quick, swarming defense that looked like the traffic outside Herschel's hotel room. The Nittany Lions made life miserable for Herschel almost all evening. Not counting the Clemson game, when his thumb was in a cast, Herschel was held to his lowest total of the season—103 yards on 28 carries. He also played the last few minutes after his left shoulder had popped out—as it had in the Sugar Bowl game two years earlier.

Penn State rode Blackledge's passing arm and Warner's lightning sweeps and slants from start to finish. The Lions pounced on the Dawgs early, then held on for a 27–23 victory that gave coach Joe Paterno his first national championship.

"They went out and played like champs," Herschel said. "They'd get my vote for national champion."

Herschel would now have a chance to run without having to dodge tacklers—on the indoor track circuit. At New York's Millrose Games, he beat out a number of the world's leading sprinters in the 60-yard dash heats, and in the final he was a close runner-up to Ron Brown in a blistering finish.

When he wasn't going to school or running track, Herschel was busy accepting awards around the nation. When he was in Philadelphia for the Maxwell Award, he spoke of money and life. "Money is not what I'm looking for out of life," he said. "Money is great, and I reckon it's super to have, but that's not what I want. I want to be happy. Happiness for me is competing."

He found happiness in another way, too. Soon the news was official that Herschel and Cindy DeAngelis would become a team. On the day after Valentine's Day, 1983, Herschel and Cindy were engaged to be married—sometime in 1984, after Herschel's graduation, her parents said. Claude Felton, director of

**Herschel picks up yardage, but not enough to beat Penn State in the Sugar Bowl.**

the Georgia sports information office, added, "It's not something that's going to happen right away. They won't be eloping on us."

The couple had been dating about three years, and Herschel had given Cindy a diamond engagement ring during the 1982 football season.

Their shared interests—a zest for sports and a strong faith in God—would help them see beyond their differences. Theirs would be both an interfaith and interracial marriage. He is Baptist and black; she is Catholic and white. Cindy, who is a year older than Herschel, was then majoring in business at the University of Georgia.

"I know a lot of people don't accept things," Cindy told *USA Today*. "But if the world is going to change for the best, people are going to have to do something about it. I never was prejudiced, and I never will be. God said He created everybody equal. His word is good enough for me."

On February 16, the day after Herschel's engagement announcement, he canceled an appearance at an awards dinner in Buffalo. There, he was to have been honored as the "top amateur athlete" at the eleventh annual Dunlop Pro-Am Awards Dinner. It was reported that Herschel had the flu.

At that point began one of the most eventful weeks in the history of American sports. It would be a week of confusion, contradiction, and controversy.

It all started on February 16, 1983, when Herschel met privately in the Athens Holiday Inn with J. Walter Duncan, Jr., an Oklahoma City oil tycoon who owned the New Jersey Generals of the newly formed USFL.

There, according to reports published later, Duncan offered—and Herschel signed—a multimillion-dollar contract early in the evening of February 17 to play for the Generals. Published estimates of the sum ranged from $5 million to $16.5 million, including fringe benefits. However, Duncan also offered Herschel an escape clause—meaning that Herschel could back out of the contract by the next morning.

Herschel did—just two hours after he had signed. At 11 o'clock the same evening, Herschel changed his mind and told Duncan he wanted out of the contract.

The next day the news media were filled with reports that Herschel had been offered as much as $16.5 million by the Generals. Herschel immediately called a news conference on the Georgia campus. He told reporters he would play his final season of eligibility at Georgia in 1983. He denied ever having seen a contract. "I've heard $16.5 million, $15.9 million, but there never was an offer," Herschel said. "All I know is I didn't see a contract. I hadn't signed 'cause I think I'd be gone if I had signed."

But hours later the Boston *Globe* reported that

114

Herschel had indeed signed a contract and then backed down. If the report was true, Herschel's days as a college football star were over. He would be ineligible under NCAA rules—even if he had merely *discussed* with any pro team how much money he would be paid.

Did Herschel sign? Questions mounted all weekend. So did the pressure. There was pressure on the NCAA to investigate. There was pressure on Herschel to clear the air.

By Monday, February 21, NCAA officials decided to investigate. They found out that Herschel had indeed violated regulations by signing a contract. It didn't matter, the NCAA said, that Herschel had also backed out of the contract. Either way, Herschel was now ineligible and could no longer play college football.

The world learned that Herschel Walker had broken his promise to stay in college. He would leave Georgia to play professional football for the New Jersey Generals. Team president Duncan wrote Herschel a check—his bonus for signing—for $1.5 million. Herschel gave the check to his mother, who deposited it in the Bank of Wrightsville.

Herschel's attorney, Jack Manton, read a statement from Herschel to reporters: "I wish to apologize to coach Dooley, the University of Georgia, and all the people that have been my loyal friends. I ask you for your forgiveness and ask God for His forgiveness."

Herschel's changeover from collegian to pro happened almost too fast for anyone—even Herschel—to grasp. The state of Georgia was in a state of shock. Somebody good-humoredly placed a classified ad in the Atlanta *Journal-Constitution* under Missing Pets: "LOST one bulldog, 240 lbs., answers to the name of Herschel."

"Does everybody in Georgia still hate me?" Herschel asked in Orlando, Florida, where he'd arrived in team owner Duncan's private plane. "I hope not," Herschel went on. "Please tell everyone in Georgia not to hate me."

His arrival by helicopter at the Generals' practice field at the University of Central Florida looked like something out of the movies. About two hundred reporters and TV crews, some from as far away as New York, had swooped onto the scene.

Now, as Herschel turned 21, he looked ahead—to his professional debut and that of the 12-team United States Football League. There was little doubt that Herschel could make it, but could the USFL? The new league would be playing its games from the first week of March to mid-July—in competition with baseball, barbecues, and vacations.

But the league was well financed, mostly with a multimillion-dollar ABC television contract. Actors Burt Reynolds and Lee Majors were part owners.

And the USFL had Herschel Walker. League owners were counting on him to draw the crowds to the stadiums, attract millions more via television, and make the headlines just as he had as a college hero in Georgia.

# 12

# GENERAL WALKER

During the mid-1970s, America had watched another summer football league go down in flames. The World Football League had lasted only two seasons.

Now America watched again—this time with college football's most celebrated player in years running against teams stocked with might-have-beens and has-beens.

Herschel's debut was perhaps the most widely publicized of any pro football player's since 1925, when Red Grange, the University of Illinois' "Galloping Ghost," signed with the Chicago Bears and played in exhibition games around the country.

Herschel first suited up in white-and-red New Jersey uniform number 34 in the Los Angeles Coliseum, scene of the 1984 Olympics. "I still want to go to the Olympics," Herschel told reporter Sam Skinner. He hoped that hurdler Renaldo Nehemiah (a San Francisco 49er receiver) would set a precedent by winning

**General Walker looks for an opening in his new role as a professional.**

his challenge for the right to compete in the Olympics in one sport while earning a living in another.

"I still think the decision in favor of Nehemiah is gonna come through," Herschel said. "I'd love to be in the starting blocks here in the finals. I know if I won't be in the blocks, I'll be here watching."

A crowd of 34,002, only about a third of the Coliseum's capacity, showed up to watch Herschel run against the Los Angeles Express. It was the smallest crowd of any USFL opener on that Sunday afternoon in March. Millions more watched on television.

The first time Herschel carried the ball, he swept right end, smoothly hurdling a couple of fallen players, and got 9 yards. It would be his longest gain of the day. Three carries later, nobody touched him as Herschel skirted right end for 5 yards and his first professional touchdown. By the end of the first quarter, Herschel had racked up 38 yards on 9 carries. It began to look like an instant replay of those autumn afternoons in Georgia.

After that, however, Herschel found very little daylight—and few more opportunities to run. He finished with only 65 yards on 16 carries as the Generals lost to L.A., 20–15. Herschel was watching from the sidelines when the Generals threatened to pull the game out at the finish.

The Generals drove to the L.A. 5, only to be stopped when L.A. nose guard Eddie (Meat Cleaver) Weaver,

Herschel's ex-Georgia teammate, threw quarterback Bobby Scott for a 9-yard loss. "Every time they came to the line, I was looking for Herschel," Weaver said afterward. "I never saw number 34. We were all looking for him."

Why didn't coach Chuck Fairbanks send Herschel in? "Well, I don't know," Fairbanks said lamely. "I really don't have an answer for that." Then he added, "Give him a break—he's only been here for a week."

Herschel didn't have many answers, either. But he was gracious in defeat, considering how little practice he'd had at it (at Georgia, he'd lost only three times in 36 games). "It's tougher out there than I thought it would be," he said. "A lot of the guys had more speed than I expected to see. Besides the speed, the execution was better than I'm used to seeing. That's the biggest adjustment I have to make."

It turned out that Herschel had other adjustments to make. His New Jersey line didn't block nearly as well as the one he ran behind at Georgia. He got only 60 yards on 13 carries and fumbled twice in a 25–0 loss to Philadelphia. He also was upstaged by Philadelphia's Kelvin Bryant, a rookie from North Carolina, who rushed for 114 yards. "I don't know," Herschel said afterward. "I could be trying too hard."

When the Generals made their home debut, a league-record crowd of 53,370 showed up at Giants Stadium in East Rutherford, New Jersey. The game was a huge letdown for the home fans, who booed and jeered the Generals to a 32–9 loss to the Tampa Bay Bandits. But it was an even bigger disappointment for Herschel, who had only 39 yards on 19 carries to show for an afternoon's work.

"I don't know what I'm doing right or wrong," he said. "I'm still learning. In this league, football is a lot different from college."

Even the Chicago Bears' star running back, Walter Payton, joined the critics of New Jersey's blockers. "Maybe the offensive line has heard so much about Herschel Walker they think he can do it on his own," Payton said. "My advice to Walker is to keep his head up and not let a few bad games get him down."

Things turned from bad to worse for Herschel the following week. Not only did the winless Generals lose their fourth in a row (31–21 to the Boston Breakers), but Herschel fumbled three times, losing the ball twice. His last fumble—with the score at 21–21—set up a go-ahead-for-keeps field goal by Boston.

"I really don't know how it happened," said Herschel, who did gain 97 yards on 21 carries and caught four passes for another 62 yards. "I had both hands on the ball and it just sort of popped out."

But there were good times, too. Wedding bells rang for Herschel and Cindy on March 31, 1983. They were married in an unannounced ceremony by the mayor of Bloomingdale, New Jersey, in the home of the father of Cindy's bridesmaid.

Marriage apparently agreed with Herschel. Three nights later, Herschel ran the way he did at Georgia, piling up 177 yards and three touchdowns on 33 carries at Arizona as the Generals won their first game ever, 35–21.

"It's a relief just to win a game," Herschel told the press afterward. "This is a night when we started to click. Nothing was different for me." Then he added good-naturedly: "I'm just the same good-looking Herschel."

Herschel had plenty else to smile about besides his marriage to Cindy and his big game against the Arizona Wranglers. He signed a long-term contract to lend his signature to footballs and other sports equipment as part of Franklin Sports Industries' "superstar advisory staff," which included ex-boxer Sugar Ray Leonard, baseball slugger Mike Schmidt, and retired quarterback Joe Namath. Earlier, Herschel agreed to wear and endorse Adidas athletic shoes— under a 10-year contract that is believed to bring him between $1 million and $2 million.

"I'm planning to live to be 165," Herschel joked with his engaging smile, "and make fourteen hundred million dollars."

Now Herschel stayed in high gear. He powered for 133 yards on a rainy Sunday in New Jersey even though the Generals lost to Michigan, 21–6, before only 17,648 fans. Then came a 142-yard game in a 23–22 triumph over the Washington Federals, and 138 yards in a 17–14 overtime loss to the Chicago Blitz.

His next stop was Denver, where Herschel ran wild in a 34–29 win over the Denver Gold. A crowd of 47,940 watched him twist and spin and dive for 172 yards in his most dazzling day yet as a professional. What's more, he surpassed Kelvin Bryant of Philadelphia and became the USFL's first rusher to gain more than 1,000 yards.

The game-breaker came midway through the final quarter. Herschel crashed at the middle, flattened one Denver tackler, then quickly changed directions and raced by everybody 80 yards to a touchdown, his longest run since high school.

Twelve hundred miles away, in Alpharetta, Georgia, Herschel's old coach, Gary Phillips, sat at home, watching the game on television. Just when Herschel broke into the open field, Phillips muttered, "See ya later!"

"What did you say, Gary?" his wife, Barbara, called from the next room.

"I said, 'See ya later!'" Phillips repeated.

"See ya later!" is what Phillips used to say when Herschel ran away from everybody, in Johnson County. It was just like old times.

# Epilogue

Herschel Walker has made millions of Americans take a closer look at the sometimes fuzzy distinction between amateur and professional athletes. He also will be remembered as the athlete who changed the course of football history.

By leaving college one year early to turn professional, he put football on the same footing with several other sports.

Magic Johnson left Michigan State's 1979 NCAA championship basketball team before his class graduated to sign a multimillion-dollar contract with the Los Angeles Lakers. Jimmy Connors and John McEnroe made early departures from UCLA and Stanford, respectively, in the 1970s to play professional tennis. Wayne Gretzky became a professional hockey star while still in his teens. And baseball has had countless players—including pitcher Bob Feller in the 1930s—who signed pro contracts as teenagers.

No one told these athletes they had to wait until

four years after high school before they were allowed to turn professional. Herschel himself questioned why it should be different for football players. And he took a giant step farther by signing with a league that made him an exception to the rule that prohibits the signing of underclassmen.

Putting all that controversy aside, Herschel Junior Walker is a symbol of the changing South. Had he come along more than a decade ago, when there were no black football players at Georgia, Herschel might have left the South and ended up in a Big Ten backfield or in a West Coast school. Or he might have gone to a predominantly black college like Grambling or Florida A & M.

Had he come along before they integrated the schools in Johnson County, Georgia, not quite two decades ago, Herschel never would have become a football player. In those days Doc Kemp High, the former all-black school in Wrightsville, couldn't scratch up enough money to field a football team.

Even if Herschel hadn't kicked a football or shot a basketball or faced the starter's gun, he probably would have excelled in something. He was winning 4-H Club contests long before he could beat his sister in footraces. "Evidently, somewhere along the way, he decided he was going to be somebody," said Schuyler Reynolds, his high school guidance counselor.

Herschel's three-year contract with the Generals will take him through the 1985 USFL season. That's assuming the league will last that long. Whether it survives or not, Herschel will be in a position to pick his NFL team and perhaps return home as a member of the Atlanta Falcons.

More important, in the eyes of football fans everywhere, Herschel Junior Walker would then have a chance to display his remarkable talents in the league of the Super Bowl. And go down in history as one of the greatest football players of all time.

# About the Author

Jeff Prugh is an Atlanta writer who was the southern correspondent for the Los Angeles *Times* and an ABC News consultant. Previously, he was an award-winning *Times* sportswriter based in Los Angeles.

His work has also appeared in *TV Guide, Time, Sports Illustrated,* and *Pro!* as well as *Best Sports Stories*.

A native of Pittsburgh, Pennsylvania, Mr. Prugh began his career at eighteen on the Glendale, California, *News-Press* and was president of the University of Missouri School of Journalism's class of 1962.

He is also co-author of *The List*, a book on the Atlanta murders, and is co-author of *The Wizard of Westwood*, a biography of former UCLA basketball coach John Wooden.